ZONE PRESS

VARIATIONS
for

WINNING BASKETBALL

ZONE PRESS

VARIATIONS FOR

WINNING BASKETBALL

by
Cliff Ellis

Parker Publishing Company, Inc.
West Nyack, New York

Library of Congress Cataloging in Publication Data

Ellis, Cliff.
   Zone press variations for winning basketball.

   1. Basketball--Defense. I. Title.
GV888.E54   796.32'32   74-22286
ISBN 0-13-984054-0

Printed in the United States of America

To Carolyn, a lovely wife and mother to whom I owe much of my success, and to my wonderful daughter, Chryssa De Anne.

ACKNOWLEDGEMENTS

To my wonderful parents, Robert and Connie, for their love and understanding. Thank you, Randy, Carolyne, and Teresa, for helping me enjoy a great childhood.

To Robert Trammell, my great friend, who is coaching at the University of South Alabama, for his encouragement and friendship during my college and coaching career. Thank you, Kay, for your friendship.

To Jimmy Earle, Head Basketball Coach at Middle Tennessee State University, for his friendship and encouragement in writing this book.

To Ron Shumate, Head Basketball Coach at the University of Tennessee at Chattanooga for teaching me different phases of basketball when I was his assistant. Thank you, Mickey, for being so great.

To my assistant coaches, Paul Carr and Herman Swain, for their hard work and dedication.

To Grover Hicks, Bobby Walton, and Bobby Welch, coaches that I have worked with during my high school coaching career, for their friendship and encouragement.

To my former principals, Leon Rogers, Colly V. Williams, and Ashley Hutcheson, for their guidance and encouragement.

To Phillip Rountree, who taught me various sports when I was a child and who has followed my coaching career closely, giving me much encouragement.

To Dr. Ernest L. Stockton, President of Cumberland College, for his wholehearted support and interest in the basketball program.

To Jimmy Parker, wherever you are, and Freddie Hall, for teaching me to play the game hard and fair.

To my grandmothers, Pauline Carlton and Gertrude Ellis, for their love and understanding.

Your Guide to Zone Press Variations

The zone press has helped my teams establish a 129-16 record over a six-year period. As a unit of our multiple defense, it gives us a different look and a different weapon to upset the offense.

During those times in a game when we employ our zone presses, we have forced our opponents to commit sixteen to seventeen turnovers while allowing an average of only two or three baskets. This gives us a big advantage over the opponents, and they must really hang tough to beat us. One of my fondest memories goes back to a season at Vanguard High School in Ocala, Florida, when we were playing one of our arch rivals in our last home game of the year. We started four juniors and one sophomore, who was our biggest man at six feet, three inches. We used the zone press the entire ball game and caused twenty-three turnovers against a very strong ball club and won the game 61-60. If we had not pressed, they would have blown us out of the gym. In that same season we had a team at the end of the first quarter 30-8 because of our zone press variations. During one season, while at Niceville High School, my team held an opponent to twenty-nine points in a game. This particular opponent was an AAAA school, which is the largest classification for high school teams in Florida. The most successful night in making the opponent turn the ball over occurred in our homecoming game, and the biggest crowd ever at a Vanguard basketball game was on hand to see us play. We caused thirty-one turnovers, were up 55-28 at the half, and won by a final score of 109-55. *Zone Press Variations for Winning Basketball* relates to the basketball coach the method we use to achieve this particular unbelievable efficiency.

From a survey I took of various coaches, I have found that most coaches spend the majority of their practice time on their half court offenses, which does not include attacking the press. These coaches spent very little time on attacking the press and many of them felt this was their weakest area pertaining to basketball. This book will show the coach how to successfully teach and win with zone press variations.

Zone Press Variations for Winning Basketball contains step by step diagrams and illustrations that will show how to teach every type of zone press: the full court zone press, the three-quarter court zone press, and the half court zone press. The book tells how to align the personnel in each of these presses. A way to disguise the zone press so that it will keep opponents confused is also covered. Methods of regrouping a team if another team breaks the zone press so that they cannot score are explained thoroughly. Individual and basic fundamental defense is also covered so that the coach can teach the zone press more effectively. Various drills are diagrammed and illustrated to facilitate perfecting the zone presses.

Zone Press Variations for Winning Basketball contains maneuvers I have used during my six successful years of coaching. The press variations will provide coaches with every possible look on defense. This creates a grave problem for the opponents. How does a team counter so many defenses in a ball game? The book gives the coach of a weaker team the capability of beating a stronger team by keeping his opponent from playing the type of game he wants to play and forcing him into making numerous turnovers throughout the game.

C.E.

TABLE OF CONTENTS

9

ZONE PRESS

VARIATIONS
for

WINNING BASKETBALL

Chapter 1
Shaping the Zone Press

The zone press, one of the most potent weapons in basketball, is the primary reason that I have been able to win. Throughout my tenure in coaching basketball at all levels, I have found many reasons why I believe that the zone press has helped me become successful.

One of the main reasons we use the zone press is that it confuses the opponent. We have yet to find a team that is totally prepared to combat our variety of presses in a ball game. We may be in a full court zone press one minute and then change to a half court zone press. It is possible that we will use ten different types of presses on an opponent in one ball game. This has thrown opponents off many times. They get to a point where they will completely lose their composure and blow up. In one ball game I recall a team that was hurting one of our full court zone presses. They were leading by seven points when we changed to a three-quarter court zone press. They still held onto their lead so we changed again to a half court zone press. Boom! It was all over. By changing the zone presses we found a press they were not ready for. We won the game by eleven points.

I have found that teams spend little or no time combating all of the presses and therefore, we confuse the opponents by throwing many different zone presses at them. By using a variety you will keep the opponent guessing. This creates problems for the opponent. I have talked to players from opposing teams and they felt that they were worrying about what press we were in and what tactics to use to beat it. It took their thoughts away from the other phases of the game.

The zone press keeps control or semi-control teams from playing their game. They must play ours. Usually the control teams like to play a slow game and work for that good shot. We are going to press these teams when they get off the bus and not let them run their offense. These types of teams usually spend more than fifty per cent of their practice time working on their controlled offense. Thus, we are going to make them do things in a game that they are not practiced in.

Players like a press that is clicking. Today's players like the fast game. They want to move. By pressing they are constantly playing a fast game. It also provides them with the opportunity to score more often. After a steal is made it usually allows them to take the easiest shot there is—the layup.

The zone press allows a team that is behind ten or twelve points to come back quickly. Many times my teams have been down in the late stages of the game by ten to fifteen points and have come back to win. In one game we made up a deficit of ten points within forty-five seconds through the use of the zone press. All it takes is a few steals to be back in the game.

By *using* the various zone presses a team will acquire a great deal of knowledge about *breaking* zone presses. Through utilizing these presses players will know what to expect when other teams press them. A coach will be better prepared than most other coaches because he will know the strengths and weaknesses of the various zone presses and his team will be better prepared in attacking them.

Spectators love it. There is nothing more exciting to a fan than seeing his team steal the ball from the opponent and laying it into the basket for two points. They like action and movement and by utilizing the zone presses they will definitely get the action they came for. At the end of the season at Vanguard High School in Ocala, Florida, the attendance had tripled itself from the year before. One of the main factors in the increase in attendance was that we utilized various zone presses and the fans loved to see this action thirty-two minutes of the game. It was fast and exciting basketball.

Another reason for using zone presses is that the good ball handler must handle two defensive players. This trapping prevents a team with one tremendous ball handler from bringing the ball up the floor by himself. He will be doubled teamed and not allowed to bring it up. Another player will also handle the ball, and hopefully will commit many turnovers throughout the game.

My teams are taught that they must constantly be aggressive to win. Defense is the key. If we are going to win, we must play defense. We must attack our opponents defensively like a hungry dog would go after his bone. This, fellow coaches, is exactly what the zone press is all about. It will make players be aggressive if they like to win because if a team is not aggressive when pressing it will be blown out of the gym. This aggressiveness on the floor is of great carry over value to our bench. If a player on the bench sees aggressiveness played when we are pressing, he will go into a game with this same fire when he is called to substitute. On the other hand, if a non-aggressive team is on the floor a substitute is more apt to go into the game with this same attitude. Making a team be aggressive can be achieved through utilizing the various zone presses.

The zone press can help a team overcome bad shooting nights. Any team who plays a twenty, twenty-five, or thirty game schedule can expect to have a bad shooting night. This is really when the zone press comes in handy. Defense is the only way a team can win when these nights occur. Therefore, this team must rely on making the other team turn the ball over numerous times to make up for a bad shooting night. The zone press can cause thirty to forty turnovers a game and this definitely can offset those "off" nights.

THE PLAYER'S ROLE FOR A SUFFICIENT ZONE PRESS

The mental condition of a basketball team is of utmost importance. If a player has the desire to win, he will win because he will put forth his maximum effort in practice and games. If a player believes in himself he will come through under pressure. If a player is not stubborn, he will be more interested in the good of the team rather than himself. If a player is dedicated, he will perform off the floor as well as on the floor. If a player will accept criticism, he will become better skilled in the game.

If teams are going to win, they must have the right mental attitude. Good team morale is a necessity. I have seen many teams fail because of a lack of it. I have always believed that *you don't put morale on like a coat—you build it day by day.*

Being a basketball player does not imply merely wearing the uniform and being a member of the team. There are many more important phases to think about if a player is going to be a winner —not only in basketball but in life as well. Through my coaching experience and through learning from other coaches in the game, I have compiled the following list of qualities that are absolutely necessary for each of the basketball players. Each year when I recruit and look for members for my squad I look for these qualities. They are characteristics necessary for a championship basketball team and qualities that I look for when I am trying to find players that fit my philosophy of pressing.

- First, the player must be coachable. He must be able to take coaching. The complete basketball player can take criticism and does not look for excuses.
- A basketball player must be willing to work hard in practice to attain winning results in a basketball game. He must put forth one hundred per cent every day.
- The true basketball player wants to win badly. It kills him to lose, and he does not mind skinning a knee to go after a loose ball.
- A person who conditions both on and off the floor has a quality of the super basketball player. Conditioning is tough and the responsibility is heavy.
- Coming through under pressure is another quality of a good basketball player. The player must forget about past mistakes, past success, or a bad call and work on what he is doing at the time. A basketball player who will play every second as if it is his last is someone who can come through under pressure.
- Wanting to improve is a desire of a good basketball player. An outstanding player will work twice as hard practicing things he cannot do well. A player must be willing to practice long and hard at accomplishing a skill he is weak in.
- A player that can press is a player that believes in his team and his coach. He knows that if a coach gets on him it is to help him become a better player. A player that has never been criticized by a coach is probably a loser.

I have never known a great athlete who did not have confidence in himself. Every player on our team must believe that the press is going to work and that he is going to see that it will. Confidence is a major characteristic that each of the members of our squad must display.

Along with these qualities are the following thoughts that players must remember when priming themselves to our pressing philosophies. Each of our players is asked to study these thoughts and to believe them:

1. Behind all upsets is a greater desire to win.
2. Five men who hate to lose make a winning team.

3. Keep your temper to yourself; it's useless to others.
4. Seek perfection.
5. A fellow teammate may be faster than you; he may be a better shot; and he may be a bit taller—but he should not be your superior in TEAM SPIRIT, FIGHT, DETERMINA-TION, AMBITION, AND CHARACTER.
6. Work is often the father of pleasure.
7. The team that won't be beaten, can't be beaten.
8. All for one and one for all.
9. All the world loves a fighter; even the Devil hates a quitter.
10. Those who fly with the owls at night can't keep up with the eagles in the daytime.

Many a basketball player has failed to meet his role and make it on a basketball team because he played for himself and felt that the team could not do without him. A poem I highly regard along this line has proven to be of significant contribution to my players and their attitudes:

> Sometimes, when you're feeling important,
> Sometime, when your ego's in bloom,
> Sometime, when you take it for granted,
> You're the best qualified in the room.
>
> Sometime when you feel that your going
> Would leave an unfillable hole,
> Just follow this simple instruction
> And see how it humbles your soul.
>
> Take a bucket and fill it with water;
> Put your hand in it, up to the wrist;
> Pull it out, and the hole that's remaining
> Is a measure of how you'll be missed.
>
> You can splash all you please when you enter;
> You can stir up the water galore;
> But stop, and you'll find in a minute,
> That it looks quite the same as before.
>
> The moral in this quaint example
> Is to do just the best you can.
> Be proud of yourself, but remember,
> There's no indispensable man.
>
> Anonymous

BASIC FUNDAMENTALS OF DEFENSE

In teaching the zone press we believe that there are essential, basic elements a player must learn to make the press effective.

When teaching pressing techniques the first thing we teach is the stance. We want the feet slightly wider than the shoulders and the weight evenly distributed on the balls of the feet with one foot slightly in front of the other. The head should be erect and the eyes looking at the opponent's mid-section. We feel that by watching the area of the stomach we will not be vulnerable to fakes by the opponent because this is one section of the body that can not fake. The back should be almost straight with the shoulders parallel to the floor. The buttocks should be low to the floor. The body should be bent at the knees and not the waist. The most important thing to remember pertaining to the stance is to keep low in a crouch. After teaching the stance, we work daily on perfecting it until the player has accomplished this skill.

It is essential, after learning the correct stance, to learn to agilely move the body forward, backward, and laterally. Trapping is important in the press and these movements are necessary in making the trap work.

When teaching the player to move his body forward correctly we first emphasize the good defensive stance. We then want the player to thrust forcefully with his back foot and move his front foot forward toward the opponent with the ball. The forearms should be parallel to the floor with the elbows slightly above the knee. In teaching this we place the players in two lines on the court facing the coaches (Diagram 1-1). The players will get into a good defensive stance and, at the whistle, move forward about six or seven steps as the coaches analyze their movement.

Next, we teach our players the correct method of moving the body backwards. The player obtains a good defensive stance. He must push off the front foot very hard and at the same time step back with the rear foot. Quickness and timing are very important in this movement. Learning this step is a must because offensive players are going to take the ball to the basket. Therefore, we have to learn backward movement correctly so that we can stop this penetration. In this movement, the forearms should be parallel to the floor with the elbows slightly above the knee. As in teaching the forward body movement, we place the players in two lines and have them get into a good defensive stance and at the whistle move backwards six or seven steps

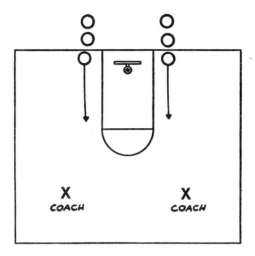

Diagram 1-1

as the coaches analyze their movements and correct mistakes.

The next step is the lateral movement. The player again obtains a correct defensive stance. If the player is to move to his left, we want him to point his left foot quickly to the direction in which he is going (Diagram 1-2), push off the right foot, and laterally slide in this direction like a boxer's shuffle without crossing the feet and keeping his feet approximately shoulder width apart. The head should stay as still as possible. The forearms should be parallel to the floor with the elbows slightly above the knee. When sliding to the right, the player pushes off the left foot quickly, points the right foot and laterally slides in this direction.

Diagram 1-2

To teach the proper lateral movement of the players, place them in three lines working with three at a time (Diagram 1-3). The players get in a good defensive stance and at the whistle laterally slide to the

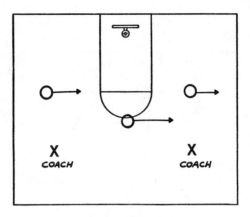

Diagram 1-3

left or right while the coaches again analyze their movements and correct their mistakes.

Once the players have accomplished the skills in stance and movement, we teach them how to guard an opponent with the basketball. Ideally, we want to force the opponent to put the ball on the floor and then make him give up this dribble as soon as possible. This helps take away the triple threat (dribbling, passing and shooting). Therefore, we tell our players that as soon as the opponent gets the ball, they must make him dribble, quickly retreat, and force him to use up the dribble. Quick movement and timing are essential. We also tell our players to study the opponent. If a player is right handed, we want to make him use his left hand as much as possible. The more he uses his weak hand, the more turnovers are likely to occur. If a player is weak left handed, for example, we want the defensive man to overplay the opponent's left side about half a step.

Talking is an important fundamental of defense. When we make the opponent give up his dribble, we must yell it out to our teammates to let them know that the dribble has been used. This will create a double team trapping situation. Talking will tell the other team members to seal off the passing lanes. Also, a defender often can harass an opponent by constantly talking to him throughout the game and can get him psychologically upset.

When guarding the man with the ball near the basket, we want the opponent to make either a bad pass or a bad shot. Harassing him is very important in making him make the bad pass.

If the opponent does attempt the shot the defender must pressure him. Many coaches neglect emphasizing stopping the shot. We want the shooter to be unable to shoot the ball the way he does in practice. We want to either get a hand on the ball when he shoots or make him move the ball away from his normal release position. Getting a hand on the ball does not necessarily mean knocking the shot into the stands, but rather it means timing the defensive jump with the opponent's jump to be able to get a hand on the ball so that the ball will not move properly in its intended flight.

We begin teaching this technique by pairing the members of the squad up according to positions. One will be an offensive man with the ball and the other the defender. The offensive man is not allowed to dribble to start with. The defensive man practices timing his jump and getting his hand on the shooter's ball. We then progress to practicing this while allowing the opponent to use one dribble. We finally progress to three dribbles. The defensive work is done daily during the pre-season, and by the time the season starts our players are pretty skilled in forcing bad shots.

We next teach our defenders to guard the man away from the ball. This is one of the most vital parts of defensive basketball.

Our first rule is to never let an opponent receive a pass within the scoring area, that is within fifteen feet of the basket. (Diagram 1-4.) We feel we are going to lose many ball games if teams get the ball in this area because of the high percentage shots made when the ball is shot from this area. We teach players to defend against this by having an offensive man try to get open in this area and by having the defensive man not let him get the ball in this area. A manager will

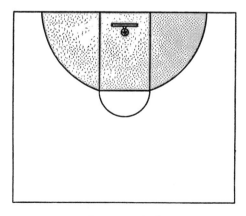

Diagram 1-4

stand at the wing area and try to feed the offensive man inside. (Diagram 1-5.) Anytime an opponent is in this scoring area the defensive player must play between his man and the ball. As the opponent moves, our player will front him.

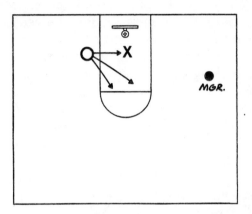

Diagram 1-5

When playing the man without the ball, the defensive player must develop good peripheral vision. A defensive man must be able to see the ball at all times. The defender must always be looking to intercept a pass or be able to pick up a loose ball. A defender playing a man without the ball must also always help a defending teammate in trouble. He should be constantly talking to his teammates letting them know what offensive maneuvers he sees the opposing team doing.

INDIVIDUAL DEFENSE

Pre-season, during the season and post season we stress individual defensive tips to our players. Listed below are some of the defensive strategies we feel are necessary to a pressing team. These individual defensive strategies are in our team notebook which each player is required to read and know.

1. Develop good peripheral vision so that you can watch both your man and the ball.
2. Always help a teammate.

3. Adjust quickly from offense to defense.
4. Keep the ball out of the scoring area.
5. Good footwork is necessary. Work diligently to improve your ability in this area.
6. Never cross your feet; use the boxer's shuffle.
7. Block your man off the board after the shot.
8. Do not relax a single second on defense.
9. Defense is determination. The champions play it.
10. Talk, talk, talk on defense.
11. It is a cardinal sin to give up the baseline.
12. Let the teammates know when the dribble has been used.
13. Keep low and in a crouch, knees bent, buttocks low, and one foot slightly in advance of the other.
14. Study your opponent constantly.
15. Never let the opponent do what he wants to do.

ONE-ON-ONE PRINCIPLES

Our next phase in teaching defense is to drill our players one against one at full court and then at half court. When teaching this, we utilize all the basic fundamentals and individual defensive tips mentioned earlier in the chapter. One of our better teaching techniques is illustrated in Diagram 1-6. We split the team into two groups; 0 is the offense and X is defense. Each group uses a lengthwise half of the floor. The offensive man will try and dribble the ball to the opposite end of the floor as quickly as possible. The defensive man's objective is to turn the offensive man as many times as he can. He tries to force the offensive man to go where he does not want to go. We want good feet movement and constant harassment of the dribbler. After the players have learned to play good defense covering half the side of the floor, we begin to operate this same one-on-one technique all over the floor (Diagram 1-7).

Next we work on one-on-one principles and techniques in the front court. A team must be able to work aggressively one-on-one when the ball is in the front court because of the danger of the opponent scoring. We start our teaching in the front court at the wing area (Diagram 1-8). In this defensive phase, we want to force the dribbler away from his objective and make him go where he does not want to go. If he wants to go left, the defender makes him go right and

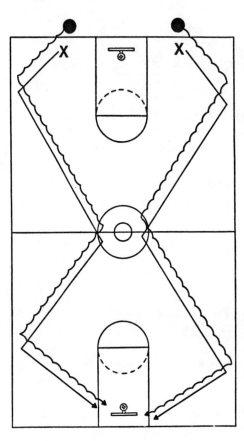

Diagram 1-6

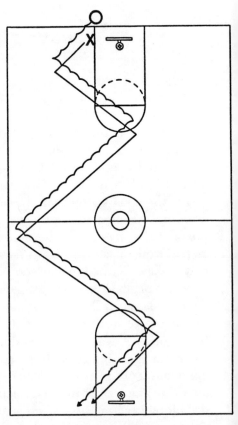

Diagram 1-7

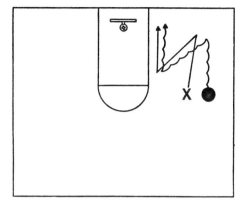

Diagram 1-8

if he wants to go right, the defender makes him go left. The player must also try to make the opponent put the ball on the floor and give up his dribble as soon as possible. Extreme pressure is put on the opponent to make him either take a bad shot or make a bad pass.

We also practice this same technique from the top of the key as shown in Diagram 1-9.

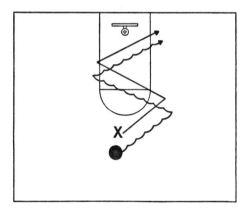

Diagram 1-9

A one-on-one situation that our players must be able to defend against in the front court is the cutter (Diagram 1-10). This is a situation that pertains to guarding the man away from the ball. As soon as the offensive man passes the ball to the wing, he usually cuts directly to the basket looking for the return pass. The defensive man must immediately jump to the inside shoulder of the offensive man and stay

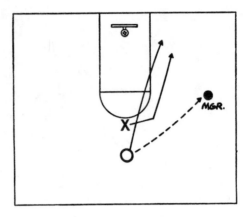

Diagram 1-10

between him and the ball as he makes his cut. The near arm should be extended to deflect passes, and the defender should be able to see both the man and the ball.

TWO-ON-TWO SITUATIONS

The next phase in teaching defense and techniques important to presses is our teaching of the two-on-two situations. We work on this at the full court level and the half court level.

In teaching the players to work two-on-two at the full court level, Diagram 1-11, we stress all of the defensive fundamentals that were

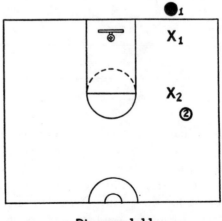

Diagram 1-11

taught in the one-on-one phase and add just a little bit more. We now emphasize contesting the inbounds pass. The defensive man, X1, is to put as much pressure on the inbounds passer, 01, as possible. The defensive man, X2, is to front the inbounds receiver, 02, and try to keep him from getting the inbounds pass. If he intercepts the pass, the defensive men try to convert the steal into a score. If 02 receives the inbounds pass, X2, must apply his one-on-one techniques turning the dribbler as often as possible and forcing him away from his objective. As soon as he can make 02 give up the ball, it is X1's job to cut off the passing lane to 01. (Diagram 1-12.)

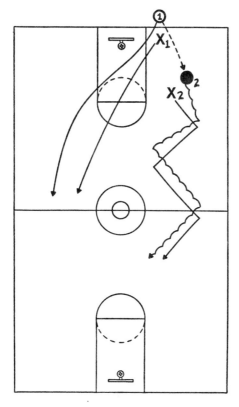

Diagram 1-12

After working at the full court level there are important defensive techniques that must be taught in order to combat basic offensive maneuvers in the front court. These are the "pic 'n roll," "give 'n go," and the shuffle cut.

The "pic 'n roll," Diagram 1-13, must be defended against. We want the defensive man on 01 to beat 01 to the pick and not allow him to get the shot. The defensive man guarding 02 is responsible for calling out the pick to 01's defender. We do not want to switch in this situation unless we have to because we do not want to have one of our guards covering a post man. The man defending 02 must stop the pass to him from 01 as he rolls to the basket.

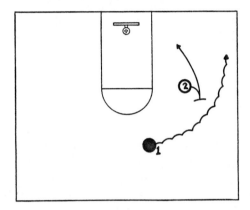

Diagram 1-13

The "give 'n go," Diagram 1-14, must also be stopped. The defender on 02 must put immediate pressure on the opponent. 01's defender must jump to his inside shoulder, as when defending the

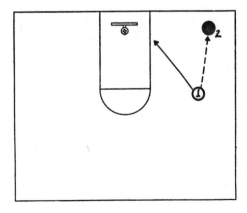

Diagram 1-14

cutter in Diagram 1-10, and play between the man and the ball, not letting the offensive man get the return pass.

The shuffle cut, Diagram 1-15, is a maneuver used in many team's offenses. 02's defender has the responsibility of telling 01's defender that the pick is being set. 01's defender immediately jumps to the side of the ball, playing between the man and the ball and not letting the pass come to the cutter. It is important that 01's defender beat his opponent to the pick set by 02 so he can go over the pick to the side of the ball. If he goes behind the pick away from the ball, the cutter will be able to receive the ball in the scoring area. This is one of the cardinal sins of defense. Again, 01 and 02's defenders do not switch unless it is absolutely necessary.

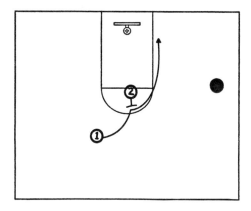

Diagram 1-15

THREE-ON-THREE TECHNIQUES

Another phase in our defensive teaching program is the three-on-three techniques. We stress the same techniques that were used in the one-on-one and two-on-two situations. We now increase the group work adding more people. We start with six people, three on offense and three on defense, utilizing the full court level (Diagram 1-16). We line up two offensive men (02, 03) at the free throw line side by side and have two defensive men (X2, X3) fronting them. X1 applies pressure on 01, the inbounds passer, and X1 is told to count off the five seconds that the offensive player has to bring in the ball in hopes that it will make him hurry and make a bad pass. X2 and X3 try to intercept the inbounds pass by fronting the offensive men, 02 and

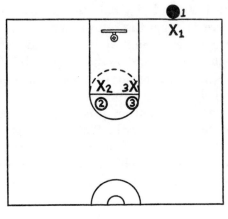

Diagram 1-16

O3. O2 and O3 screen for each other and try to break open for the inbounds pass. If the inbounds pass is completed to O3 (Diagram 1-17), X3 immediately gets between the man and the basket and uses his one-on-one principles trying to force the dribbler away from his objective, hoping he will turn the ball over or give up his dribble and make a bad pass. When X3 makes his opponent give up his dribble, X1 and X2 are taught to front their opponents and not let them receive the pass.

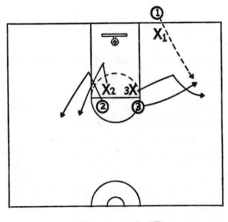

Diagram 1-17

Next we move to the three-on-three techniques that we must defend against in the front court. The basic maneuver we want to combat at this point is the split post (Diagram 1-18). This is one

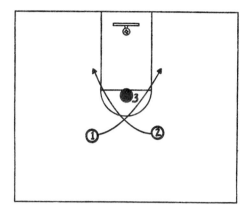

Diagram 1-18

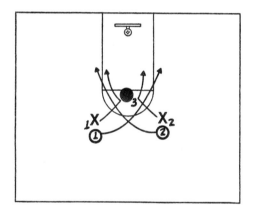

Diagram 1-19

technique that mentally is relatively easy but physically will demand a lot of work. Diagram 1-19 illustrates how to defend against this play. X3 is to play as tough as possible against 03, the offender with the ball, and not let him score. X1 and X2 are taught to beat the offenders, 01 and 02, to the post before they split. This must be done as soon as the pass is made from the outside to the post man. In this situation we will always switch defenders with the men splitting. X2 will take 01 and X1 will defend 02. The key to success with this maneuver is to beat the offenders that split to the post. Doing this successfully, allows the defenders to play defensively between the man and the ball which is a must when they are in the scoring area. We have found that if players do not automatically switch they get hung up at the post and are beaten. We also practice defending the split post at the low post areas

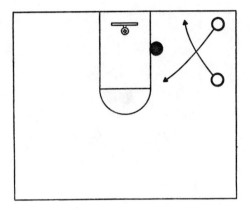

Diagram 1-20

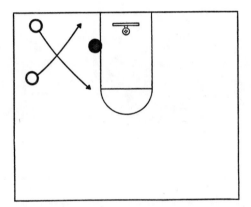

Diagram 1-21

on both sides of the goals, (Diagrams 1-20 and 1-21), and use the same techniques as at the high post.

FOUR-ON-FOUR METHODS

After completing three-on-three work, we add another offensive man and defensive man to our full court work, 04 and X4, as in Diagram 1-22. Defensive men X1, X2 and X3, use the same rules that were used in the three-on-three drills. X2 and X3 front their offenders, 02 and 03, and try to intercept the inbounds pass. X1 tries to force 01, the inbounds passer, to make a bad pass. X4, the defender

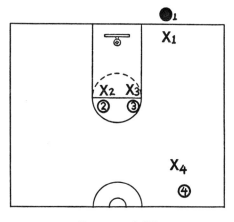

Diagram 1-22

against 04, is now brought into the picture. We allow 01, the in-bounds passer, to throw the long inbounds pass. X4 must prevent his man from getting the long inbounds pass by fronting him and staying between his man and the ball. X4 is also allowed to pick off long inbounds passes to 02 and 03, but his rule is that he must come up with the basketball. An illustration of this is shown in Diagram 1-23. If a pass is completed to any of the offensive men on the inbounds pass, the defender on the offensive receiver plays between him and the basket and tries to make him turn the ball over or give up his dribble. As soon as the dribble is given up, the three other defenders play between the man and the ball and do not let their men receive the pass.

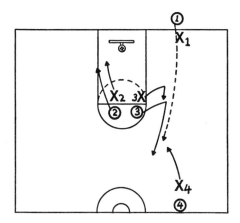

Diagram 1-23

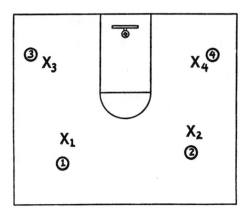

Diagram 1-24

We progress to the front court with our four-on-four situation which we call our shell game, Diagram 1-24. The offenders, 01, 02, 03 and 04, are told to free lance and execute the following offensive maneuvers: "pic n' roll," "give 'n go," cutting and driving. The defensive team, X1, X2, X3 and X4, will try to combat these maneuvers. This shell game is a very practical learning situation and has been beneficial to us especially during the season. The players love it and they will compete for windsprints that will be run after practice. The team that makes the most defensive mistakes is the loser. These mistakes are counted by the coaches.

When we progress to the four-on-four stage, we also teach what most people call ball side and help side defense as shown in Diagram 1-25. Ball side, the area 01 and 03 are in, is the side of the floor that

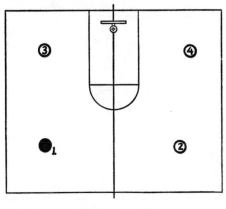

Diagram 1-25

the ball is on and where the offensive team is trying to maneuver. Help side, the area 02 and 04 are in, is the side of the floor that is away from the ball. Defensive men on the ball side of the floor must play their men tight. We tell the defensive men who have opponents on the help side to sag toward the ball away from their opponents and help any teammate who is beaten by the offensive man. Defenders on the help side must always help out until the ball comes to their side of the floor.

Chapter 2
Principles and Reasons for Incorporating Man-To-Man Defense with the Zone Press

The man-to-man defense is the basic standard defense my teams have used for the past six years. We feel that this defense has played a major role in the success of our zone presses. We always begin a ball game playing strictly a man-to-man defense either at the half court, three-quarter court, or full court level. We do this to see what kind of offensive set a team is going to attack us with. After a few times down the floor, we know what type of offensive set the opponent is using and we can decide what type of zone press we want to use. For example, if we are in our half court man-to-man defense, which we call our delay attack, and a team uses a 2-1-2 offensive set (Diagram 2-1), we use our audibles changing from our half court man-to-man defense to our 2-1-2 half court zone press. The defensive alignments are the same for each (Diagrams 2-2 and 2-3); therefore, we will alternate the defense and hope that we have disguised our zone press through the use of a half court man-to-man defense.

An example of this same technique at the three-quarter court is shown in Diagrams 2-4 and 2-5. When the opponent uses a 2-2-1 offensive set in attacking our man-to-man defense, we use our audibles to call for our 2-2-1 three-quarter court zone press on the hopes that we can cause turnovers by keeping the opponent thinking we are always in a man-to-man defense. When we suddenly change to the

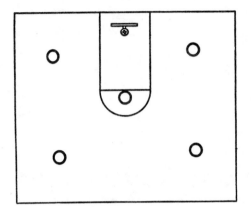

Diagram 2-1

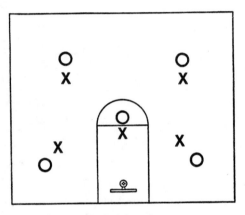

Diagram 2-2
Man-to-Man Half
Court Defensive Alignment

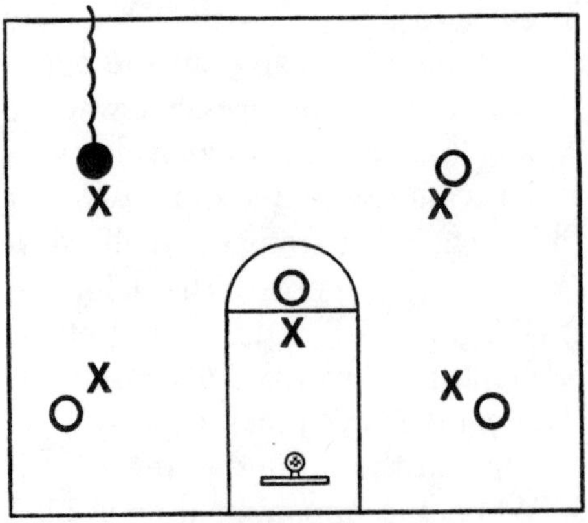

Diagram 2-3
2-1-2 Half Court
Zone Press Alignment

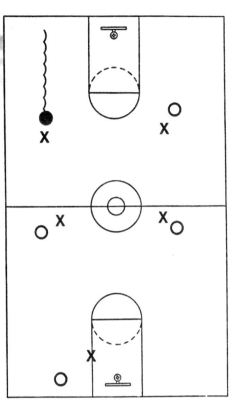

Diagram 2-4
Three-Quarter Court
Man-to-Man Defense

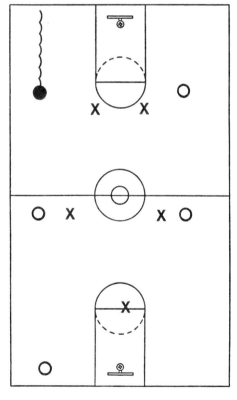

Diagram 2-5
2-2-1 Three-Quarter Court
Zone Press Alignment

zone press and start trapping, it baffles them and we get the ball through numerous steals and turnover mistakes made by the opponent.

The offensive set that the opponent uses to attack us with determines the type of zone press we use, but we hope that our man-to-man defense hides the zone press.

We also like to incorporate the man-to-man defense with our zone press because, as in the zone press, every man has a job that he must do and if he fails the team will fail. If the man a defender is guarding beats him, the finger can be pointed at the defender. There is no second guessing as to who hurt you if an opponent scores. This challenge of defense against offense puts fire and aggressiveness into a defensive player and has proven to be of carry over value to our zone presses.

Man-to-man defense, like the zone press, forces the offensive team to attack. They cannot stand still with the basketball. The defender can force the opponent to play his type of basketball. Any time the right type of pressure is applied, a offensive team will not be able to sit on the basketball.

THE DELAY ATTACK:
HALF COURT MAN-TO-MAN DEFENSE

Our man-to-man defense is called our delay attack. We call it this because after we successfully convert a basket on offense we want to delay our pressure until the opponent crosses the half court line.

As mentioned earlier, after we see a team's offensive set, we decide what type of zone press to use. We then use audibles to constantly change our defenses from the man-to-man defense to the zone press and vice versa.

Although we simply use the man-to-man defense to disguise our zone press, the team must be skilled in the principles and techniques of our man-to-man defense to keep the offense from beating us. Whatever defense we are in we must play it tough and not let the opponent beat us.

Diagram 2-6 illustrates the defensive floor positions and responsibilities our players must use if an opponent attacks us offensively with a 2-1-2 set. It is X1's responsibility to play 01, the man with the ball, extremely tough. He tries to force him to give up his dribble so

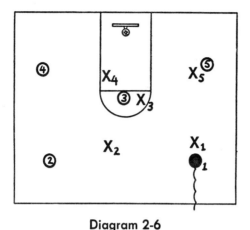

Diagram 2-6

that the other four teammates can seal off the passing lanes. X5 is on the ball side of the floor and fronts his man, 05, not letting him get the ball in the wing area. The pass from 01 to 05 is a primary pass to stop because this is where most teams' offense will initiate. We want to force them away from this objective. X3 will play between the man and the ball with his defender, 03, because 03 is in the scoring area. X2 is in a helping position because he is away from the ball and will help the defender, X1, if 01 beats him. If X1 does his job of making 01 pick up his dribble, X2 must immediately pick up his opponent, 02, and not let him receive the pass. X4 is also in a helping position because he is away from the basketball. As soon as X1 makes 01 give up his dribble, he sees that his man, 04, does not get the pass. We also tell him that since he is the farthest man from the ball he can gamble and help one of his teammates cut off a passing lane if one of them is in trouble. An example of this situation, using X3 as the defender getting beaten, is illustrated in Diagram 2-7.

Diagram 2-8 illustrates the floor positions and responsibilities of our defense when the ball is brought up the left side of the floor from a 2-1-2 offensive set.

X2 pressures the ball forcing 02 away from his objectives and tries to make him give up his dribble or turnover the ball. X1 is a helper for X2 but immediately seals off the passing lane to 01 when 02 picks up his dribble. X3 plays his opponent by being between his man and the ball, cutting off this passing lane inside. X4 is responsible for stopping the wing pass to 04. X5 is in a help position and is responsible for not letting 05 receive a pass. He also can help other teammates by sealing off a passing lane for them if one is in trouble.

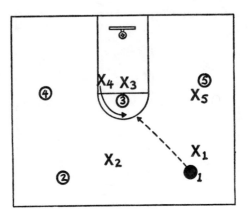

Diagram 2-7

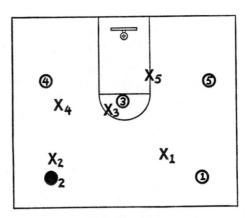

Diagram 2-8

Diagram 2-9 shows the floor assignments and responsibilities we use against teams that combat our delay attack with a 1-2-2 or 1-4 offensive set.

It is a must for X1 to turn the dribbler to one side of the floor, and not let him come down the middle. We want X1 to do this so he can have teammates in a helping position. Bringing the ball down the middle of the floor will not allow this. X1 tries to force his opponent, 01, away from his objective and cause him to make a floor mistake or to give up his dribble. The other defenders seal off the passing lanes to the opponents. X3 must cut off the wing pass to 03 by fronting him so that the opponent's offense cannot be initiated. X5's man, 05, is in the scoring area so he plays between his man and the basketball, not

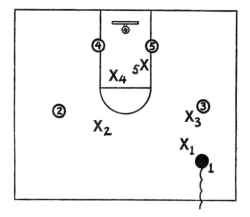

Diagram 2-9

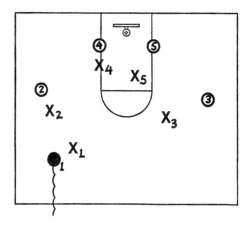

Diagram 2-10

letting the ball come in to him. X4 also has an opponent, 04, in the scoring area so he too plays between his man and the basketball. X2 is in a helping position and helps X1 stop 01's penetration if X1 is having trouble defensively. If X1 is successful in making 01 give up his dribble, X2 must stop the pass to 02.

The floor assignments and responsibilities we use against 1-2-2 or 1-4 offensive sets when the ball is turned to the left side of the floor are illustrated in Diagram 2-10.

X1 has forced the ball to the left side and forces 01 to make a turnover or give up his dribble. X2 fronts 02 sealing off the wing pass. X4 and X5 have opponents in the scoring area so they play between their men and the basketball. X3 is now in a helping position but must stop the pass to his man, 03, as soon as 01 gives up his dribble.

Diagram 2-11 illustrates the player floor positions and responsibilities used in our delay attack when opponents attack us offensively with a 1-3-1 set.

X1 must turn the dribbler down the left or right side of the floor and not let the opponent bring the ball down the middle. In this illustration X1 has turned the dribbler, 01, to the right side of the floor. He plays 01 very aggressively trying to make him give up his dribble. X4 fronts 04, cutting off the wing pass. X3 defends 03, who is in the scoring area, and plays between 03, the basketball and 01. X5's man, 05, is also in the scoring area so X5 applies the same techniques as X4. X2 is in a helping position because his man, 02, is on the side of the floor away from the basketball. He will help any teammate having defensive trouble and will cut off the passing lane to 02 when X1 makes 01 give up his dribble.

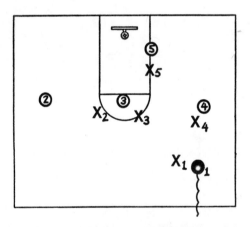

Diagram 2-11

The player floor positions used against this set when the ball is turned to the left side of the floor are shown in Diagram 2-12.

X1 pressures the dribbler, 01, hopefully causing him to make a floor mistake or pick up his dribble. X2 must stop the wing pass to 02. X3 plays between his man, 03, the basketball and 01. X5 plays 05 in the same manner. X4 is now in a helping position and is also responsible for deflecting any passes to his man, 04.

We also use zone pressing stunts in our delay attack when the ball is penetrated to the wing area. We use these techniques to keep the opponent from running its offense. We always want to force the

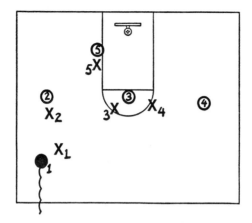

Diagram 2-12

offensive team away from its objective. We feel that most teams spend more than fifty per cent of their practice time working on their offense and we want to cause them to do things offensively that they do not practice.

When an opponent using a 2-1-2 offensive set gets the ball to the wing area, we use the techniques illustrated in Diagram 2-13. X1, upon seeing the ball passed to the wing, leaves his man to double team the offensive wing man, 05, with X5. X2, who was in a helping position, picks up 01. X3 remains with his man, 03.

X4 is the farthest man from the ball and is the key to this stunting technique. He has the responsibility of stopping the pass to the two offensive men farthest away from the ball, 02 and 04. He must watch

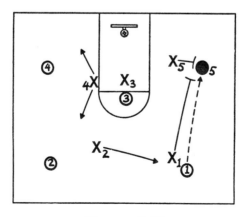

Diagram 2-13

the eyes of 05 who is intensely pressured in the double team on the basketball. Ninety-nine per cent of the time we have found that 05 will pass the ball from the double team to the men he is looking directly at because of this double team pressure situation he is in. X4 positions himself between 02 and 04, watches the passer's eyes, and anticipates intercepting the pass to either of these receivers. If one of the offenders he is guarding, 02 or 04, breaks into the scoring area, this man will be the most vulnerable receiver; therefore, X4 will pick this man up and not let him receive the pass.

Diagram 2-14 shows the techniques we use when a opponent, attacking our delay attack with a 2-1-2 offensive set, completes the wing pass on the left side of the floor. X2 releases from 02 and double teams the ball with X4. X3 stays between 03 and the basketball and 04. X5 has the responsibility of covering 01 and 05, who are the farthest removed from the ball. He plays "twixt and between" them watching the passer's eyes and taking the most vulnerable receiver. X1, who was in a helping position, picks up 02.

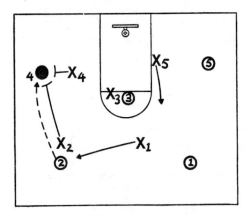

Diagram 2-14

Diagram 2-15 illustrates the zone pressing stunts we use in our delay attack when the ball is passed to the right wing from an opponent's 1-2-2 offensive set. X1 leaves his man, 01, to double team the man with the basketball, 03, with his teammate X3. X4 and X5 must remain with their men, 04 and 05, because they are in the scoring area. X2, who is the farthest from the ball and in a helping position, now must pick up the most vulnerable receiver, 01 or 02. He uses his peripheral vision to see both men, watches the passer's

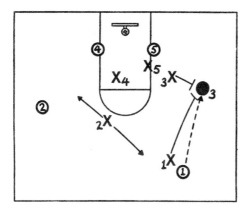

Diagram 2-15

eyes in the double team, initially plays in between 01 and 02 until he picks up who he thinks is the most vulnerable receiver of the two. This is a gamble but has proven to be very effective for us in that the variability in whom he will cover throws the opponents off balance.

Diagram 2-16 shows this technique when the ball is passed to the wing area on the left side from a 1-2-2 offensive set. X1 double teams the ball with X2. X4 and X5 play between their men, 04 and 05, and the basketball. X3 will pick up who he thinks is the most vulnerable receiver, 01 or 03.

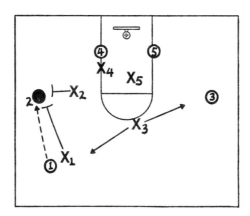

Diagram 2-16

When a team attacks our delay attack with a 1-3-1 offensive set and the ball has been passed to the wing area on the right side of the floor we use zone pressing stunts illustrated in Diagram 2-17. This

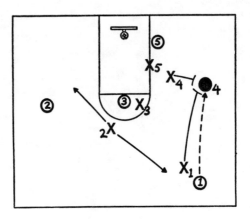

Diagram 2-17

stunt is almost identical to the stunt used against the 1-2-2 offensive set. X1 leaves 01 to double team the ballhandler, 04, with X4. X3 and X5 stay with their men, 03 and 05, and play between their men and the basketball. X2, who is farthest from the ball, will take the most vulnerable receiver, 01 or 02.

. The left side stunting technique from this set is shown in Diagram 2-18. X1 double teams the ball with X2. X3 and X5 front their men, 03 and 05, respectively. X4 picks up either 01 or 04.

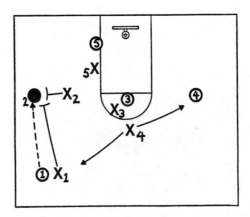

Diagram 2-18

A zone pressing stunt in our delay attack is one we use to combat an offense with the forward-to-guard handoff shown in Diagram 2-19. We picked this stunt up from Jimmy Earle, the great defensive coach

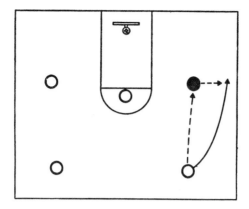

Diagram 2-19

at Middle Tennessee State University, and its techniques are illustrated in Diagram 2-20. We use this when offensive teams pass the
ball to the wing area and initiate their patterns with a forward handoff
to the guard going outside of him.

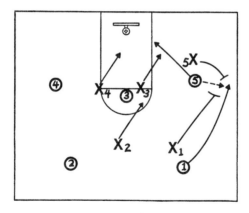

Diagram 2-20

Using a 2-1-2 offensive set to illustrate with the ball on the right
side, the defensive responsibilities are as follows: X1 follows 01 to the
ball and applies strong pressure when seeing the handoff made from
05 to 01. X5, upon seeing the handoff made, converges with X1 to
apply a strong double team on the man with the ball, 01. 05 rolls away
from the ball after making the handoff and looks for the pass. Every
team we face usually does this after a handoff. X3, the man defending

the post, is responsible for stopping the return pass to the opponent, 05, rolling to the basket. X2 drops into the high post area to prevent the pass to 03. X4, who is a helper because he has a man away from the ball, moves into the lane area and helps protect the basket. He is also told that he can gamble and pick off any passes to 02 or 04, who are off the side of the ball as long as X3 can stay with 05.

Diagram 2-21 illustrates a zone pressing stunt we use in our delay attack when an opponent with a two guard offensive set has a dribbler that turns his back to the inside of the court. The offensive guard with the ball, 01, has dribbled to his left and reversed to his right thus turning his back to the inside of the court. X2 has been watching for this key and upon seeing it double teams the opponent with X1. X5 must seal off the passing lane to 05. X3 immediately fronts his man, 03. X4 plays in between 02 and 04 but usually must immediately pick up 02 because we have found that he is the most vulnerable receiver away from the ball in this situation.

Any time the ball is passed into the scoring area from outside, all players must play aggressively, pick up their assigned men, and utilize the defensive fundamentals described in Chapter One.

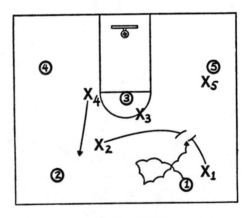

Diagram 2-21

THE REGULAR ATTACK:
THREE-QUARTER COURT MAN-TO-MAN DEFENSE

We have found that teams attack this three-quarter court pressure defense with a two man front or a one man front letting the best ball handler bring the ball up the court.

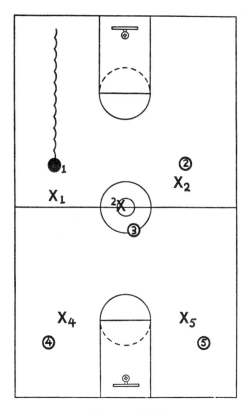

Diagram 2-22

Diagram 2-22 illustrates the floor positions and responsibilities of the defenders against a team using a two guard front to bring the basketball up the floor.

In the regular attack we are setting our opponents up for the three-quarter court zone press. Although we are setting them up, we must not lie down with this mock defense but must play it with the same fire and aggressiveness as our zone presses. After we score a basket, no defender will pick up his opposing man until he gets into the three-quarter court level (darkened space in Diagram 2-23). 01 has the basketball and X1, his defender, utilizes the one-on-one principles of forcing him away from his objectives. He tries to see that 01 makes a turnover or gives up his dribble. As soon as X1 makes 01 give up his dribble, the rule for all the other defenders in our regular attack is very simple. They must immediately front their men sealing the passing lanes off and not let them receive a pass. Learning this is mentally easy but demands aggressiveness from the players for it to

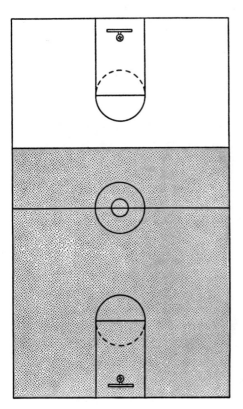

Diagram 2-23

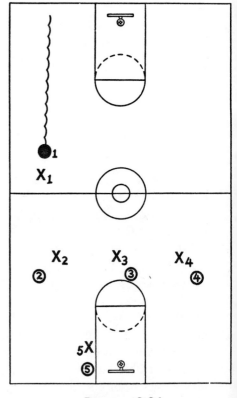

Diagram 2-24

work. If one of the five defenders eases up defensively, the whole team will suffer. X2, X3, X4 and X5 must see to it that 02, 03, 04 and 05, respectively, do not receive the pass from 01. After we have set the decoy for our zone press, we go into our 2-1-2 three-quarter court zone press.

Diagram 2-24 illustrates the techniques our defenders use when a team attacks our regular attack with a one guard front. X1 tries to cause the dribbler, 01, to make a floor mistake or use up his dribble. If he is successful in making him pick up the dribble, X2, X3, X4 and X5 who guard 02, 03, 04 and 05, respectively, front their men and do not let them receive the pass. If the ball is dribbled into half court, we utilize our basic fundamentals of individual and team defense described in Chapter One.

THE SNIPE ATTACK

A pressure defense that has proven to be beneficial to us numerous times is our snipe attack. This is our full court man-to-man pressure defense.

When we are in our snipe attack, which we use after an offensive basket, each of our men picks up his assigned man immediately and does not let him get the ball on the inbounds pass.

Most teams will attack our full court man-to-man pressure by using two men, 02 and 03, as their primary inbounds receivers (Diagram 2-25) and drop two men farther back.

The defensive alignments and responsibilities on the inbounds pass against teams that attack us with this type of set are illustrated in Diagram 2-26.

X1 harasses the inbounds passer, 01, and encourages him to make a bad inbounds pass. X2, guarding 02, and X3, defending 03, must front their opponents and not let these primary receivers receive the inbounds pass. To be successful at this they must position themselves where they can see both their men and the inbounds passer with the basketball. If our defenders, X2 and X3, play this correctly, it will force the inbounds passer to make a lob pass which we feel is the best pass to intercept. It gives X4 and X5 an opportunity to pick off a long inbounds pass to either of these men. X4 must also prevent his man, 04, from receiving the inbounds pass; therefore, he plays between his man and the basketball. We have a rule in our

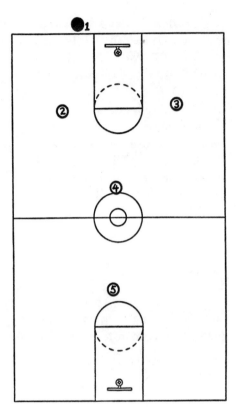

Diagram 2-25

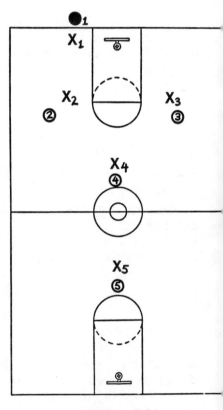

Diagram 2-26

snipe attack that allows any man who is guarding a secondary in-bounds receiver in the back court on the inbounds pass, to gamble and go for lob passes made to the primary receivers. X5 fronts 05 who is farthest from the ball on the inbounds pass and can help X4 if a long inbounds pass is made to his man, 04.

If the pass is completed to the primary receivers, Diagram 2-27, using 02 as an example, the defensive responsibilities are as follows: X2 must immediately sprint and get defensively balanced between his man, 02, and the basket. This sprinting technique will take about ten steps to catch up with the dribbler. He then utilizes his one-on-one fundamentals and tries to force the dribbler to make a floor mistake or use up his dribble. X1, X3, X4 and X5 who are guarding 01, 03, 04 and 05, respectively, immediately seal off the passing lanes to these receivers when 02 picks up his dribble. They must play between their men and the basketball.

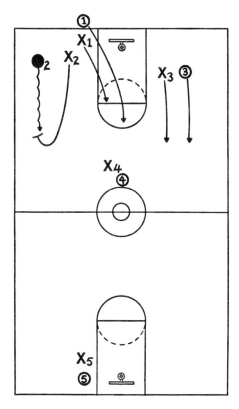

Diagram 2-27

The snipe attack won a game for us by itself during the 1972-73 season at Cumberland College. In our third game of the season we were trailing by eight points with one minute and sixteen seconds remaining on the clock. We converted a basket on offense and stole the ball three straight times converting these steals into baskets and sending the game into overtime. In the overtime, still utilizing the snipe attack, we kept stealing the ball on the inbounds pass and won the game handily. This was a big game for us because it was one of ten consecutive wins—a school record.

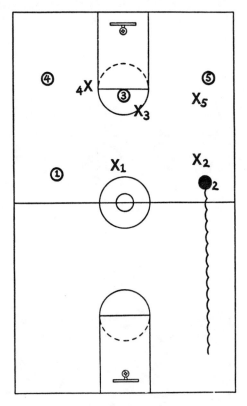

Diagram 2-28

It must be noted that when we are in the snipe attack and the opponent receives the inbounds pass and penetrates the basketball into the front court defensive techniques are the same as in the backcourt (Diagram 2-28). We will always overplay all the passing lanes when an opponent gives up a dribble. In this situation 02 has dribbled across half court and has given up his dribble. X2 puts immediate pressure on him. X1, X3, X4 and X5 seal off the passing lanes to 01, 03, 04 and 05, respectively.

Chapter 3
Techniques of the
"Slide and Trap"
Full Court Zone Press

It has amazed me for a long period of time that many coaches seldom or never use full court pressure defenses. The game of basketball is supposedly played all over the court yet I do not always see it played this way. Teams will come down the floor and score, then go back down the court to set their defense and actually play the game covering only half of the floor. Fellow coaches, this type of basketball was not meant to be and is coming to an end. For the last few years we have seen a trend away from this. Today's game involves pressure, is exciting, and fans love today's pressure game.

Most of the championship teams seen today on any level are employing full court presses. Look at the fantastic U.C.L.A. teams over the past few years. They have utilized the full court zone press very effectively. The great Florida State University team that was runner-up to U.C.L.A. in a recent N.C.A.A. tournament gained much of its prestige through the efficient use of full court pressure. Many, many more teams have enjoyed success by employing some type of full court zone press. It is part of today's game and fun to coach as well as watch.

We use the full court zone press after a successful field goal or free throw. There are various types of full court zone presses a coach can use. A coach might want to use just one type of full court zone press or he might want to use several types. The main thing to do is find the press or presses that will fit your game philosophy.

Our philosophy is to use multiple presses. We will use some type of full court zone press, three-quarter court zone press, and half court zone press virtually every ball game. Sometimes we will use only one type of each and at times we will utilize two or three variations of each. In our system, we want to keep the opponents offensive attack off balance at all times, so we utilize many presses.

Our full court zone presses are called "Slide and Trap" zone presses. The term came about through the techniques we use to double team the ball when we are in our full court zone press. To double team the ball, one of the trappers has to use a lateral slide while shifting to trap the ball and the other trapper uses what we call an advanced or forward slide. Both men use a sliding technique to trap; therefore, we gave our full court zone presses the term "Slide and Trap."

Naming the presses has certainly proved to be of incentive value to our players. The players like names attached to the presses as it gives them prestige. They feel they are the only team that is using this zone press.

The types of "Slide and Trap" full court zone presses that we use are the 1-2-1-1; 2-1-2; and the 2-2-1. Each year we have used one of these presses or all of these presses every game but it has been according to the team we were playing, the personnel we have, or the type of press a floor situation calls for.

We number our zone presses so that the players can associate a certain press with a number in case we use audibles on the floor to change our presses during a game. Audibles are called by a floor captain and he designates to the players the type of press we will use by calling out a number after a successful field goal or free throw. Our 1-2-1-1 zone presses are recognized by the number 13. The next number after 13 tells whether it will be a full court, three-quarter court, or half court zone press. Any number 2 or less is a full court zone press. So if we said thirteen, two, it would tell the players it is a 1-2-1-1 full court zone press. The following is the number system we use for our full court zone press:

1. 13-1—1-2-1-1 full court zone press without overplay on the inbounds pass.
2. 13-2—1-2-1-1 full court zone press with overplay on the inbounds pass.
3. 21-2—2-1-2 full court zone press with overplay on the inbounds pass.
4. 22-2—2-2-1 full court zone press with overplay on the inbounds pass.

ADVANTAGES OF THE FULL COURT ZONE PRESS

The full court zone press is the quickest method of getting the ball on defense and putting it into the basket. At times my teams have started a game with a full court zone press, stolen the ball a few times, and found ourselves ten points up, and the opponent literally lying down for the rest of the game. I have also seen and had teams that were ten to twelve points behind in a game apply full court zone pressure and win due to their ability to get the ball and score quickly. The quick scoring methods it provides helps you to overcome bad shooting nights and lifelessness on the court. When a team starts stealing the ball and scoring, they become aggressive and many times will get their shooting hand back through the confidence the press helped instill in the players.

Teams that try to play a control or semi-control game against a team that utilizes full court zone pressure will find it very difficult to do. Using the full court zone press will force the opponent to hurry and make him play your game.

The full court zone press eliminates letting the super player bring the ball up the floor one-on-one. Many teams with a super player will bring the ball in to this man on the inbounds pass so he can bring the ball up the floor one-on-one. The full court zone press will provide opportunity to double team this player and make him pass up the ball.

By coaching the full court zone press you will learn its techniques and strategies. Thus, when a team attacks you with a full court zone press, it will be easier for you because you will know what to expect and how to combat it through your experiences with it.

Fans love the zone press. There is nothing more exciting to a fan than seeing his team steal the ball from the opponent and score two points. We feel the zone press is one of the main reasons we have packed our gym night after night.

THE 1-2-1-1 "SLIDE AND TRAP"
FULL COURT ZONE PRESS

This is one of my favorite zone presses. We have been able to destroy opponents with this press.

The initial alignment for our 1-2-1-1 "Slide and Trap" full court zone presses is illustrated in Diagram 3-1.

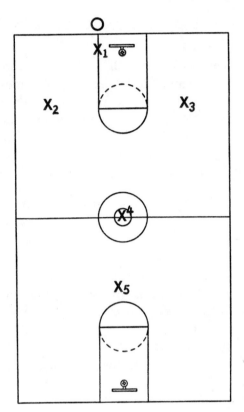

Diagram 3-1

The following are the individual characteristics and position re-sponsibilities of each defensive player in the press:

X1, the defensive point man, is our center. His long arms help prevent the long inbounds pass. He lines up on the ball and applies as much pressure as possible on the inbounds passer. He also is drilled to perfection on trapping. He will be one of the trappers and his long arms induce the lob pass from the passer, which is the easiest type of pass to intercept.

X2, the left wing, is one of our forwards. He is generally our best defensive forward because teams will usually attack to his side. His long arms will also induce the lob pass. He will trap the ball when the ball is brought in to his side.

X3, the right wing, is usually also a forward. He must be able to trap when the ball comes to his side. He should also have good lateral movement so that he can steal the ball when it is at X2's side.

X4, the middle guard, is our quickest guard. He initially lines up at the half court circle but will match up with the nearest man in his area on the inbounds pass. He is the man that will get most of the steals after a trap. He must be able to anticipate passes and be the type of player that does not mind skinning his knees to go after the ball. He is the defensive halfback of basketball. We put our quickest people (X4, X5) back because they will get most of the steals and we want our quickest men going after the passes. Our quickest men are also in the back positions because they are the best defensive men. When the press is broken we want these best defensive men back.

X5, the chance and safety man, is the other guard. His initial floor responsibility is halfway between the half court circle and the top of the key in the front court. He must stop the long inbounds pass to the deepest man, which is the safety aspect, but at the same time can free lance to intercept the ball in another area if he knows he can steal it, which is the chance aspect. He must be quick, aggressive, and a good anticipator of passes. He determines whether he can chance an interception or should stay back to protect against the long inbounds pass by the stance the opponents' inbounds passer takes to bring the ball in. If the passer is in a square stance as though he is going to throw a chest pass or bounce pass, he can move up as far as six feet above half court in order to steal an inbounds pass because as long as the inbounds passer is in this stance he cannot throw long. However, if the passer is in a baseball pass stance he must stay back and keep the nearest back man from getting the ball on the inbounds pass.

There are two things we can basically do with the inbounds pass. We can overplay all the receivers and try to intercept the inbounds pass or let them bring the ball in without pressure on the pass unless we are one hundred per cent sure we can get the steal.

The 1-2-1-1 full court zone press we use that will allow the inbounds passer to bring the ball in is called our 13-1 "Slide and Trap" zone press. Many times we will follow up our regular man-to-man attack (man-to-man without overplay as mentioned in Chapter Two) with this press. We especially like this against teams that use two men as primary receivers for the inbounds pass. We will look like we are in a man-to-man defense and hope to confuse the opponents as long as possible. (See Diagram 3-2.) In our 13-1 zone press the 1 has told us that we play behind the two primary inbounds receivers unless we are one hundred percent sure we can get the steal. We use this technique against teams with good, extremely quick guards.

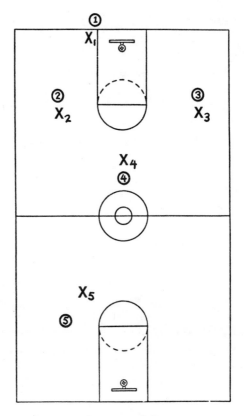

Diagram 3-2

As mentioned earlier, X2 and X3, the wing men, are our forwards and we cannot overplay the inbounds with these men efficiently against a team with extremely quick guards. Therefore, we let them have the ball on the inbounds pass unless the wing man is certain of a steal. Although X2 and X3 do not overplay, X4 and X5 must overplay and cut off the passing lanes for long inbounds pass. After the inbounds pass is made, the trapping technique becomes very important. This is illustrated in Diagram 3-3. 01 has passed the ball to 02. As soon as 02 receives the pass X2, the left wing, overplays his right hand forcing him to the middle using his left hand (most players prefer to use their right hand). Most teams like to quickly return the ball to the inbounds passer. We stop this quick return by having X1 stay with the inbounds passer until he gets to the free throw line or goes away from the ball at which time he will be picked up by another man. 02, having the passing lanes cut off, must use his

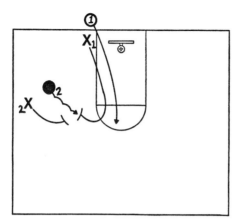

Diagram 3-3

dribble and X1, the defensive point man, and X2, the left wing, force him to give up this dribble and trap him.

Diagram 3-4 shows this same technique to the right side.

X3, forces the ball handler to the middle and traps with X1 after he has checked the inbounds passer on a quick return pass.

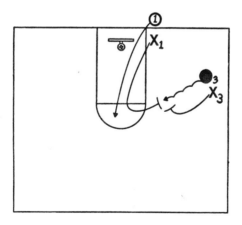

Diagram 3-4

The basic slides and player defensive coverages of our 13-1 "Slide and Trap" zone press to the left side are illustrated in Diagram 3-5.

X1, the defensive point man, stays with the inbounds passer until the opponent reaches the free throw line or goes away from the ball. (See Diagram 3-3.) He then converges with the left wing, X2, for the trap. X1 and X2 get their hands up high to induce the high lob pass.

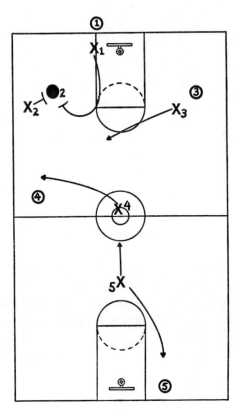

Diagram 3-5

We also tell our trappers to harass the opponent being trapped by constantly talking to him in hopes that he will panic and turn the ball over. X3, the right wing, will take any man in the area of the key looking for the interception. He will usually have to pick up the inbounds passer after X1 has stopped the quick return pass. X4, the middle guard, stops all passes to the sideline on the ball side of the floor. X5, the chance and safety man, in seeing that the ball has been trapped can now be a chance man and can come up as far as six feet above the half court line in hopes of intercepting a pass. We allow him to do this because we feel that if the trappers are doing their job it is impossible to complete a pass to an opponent near the goal. Diagram 3-6 illustrates how we show our players this technique in practice. We place two defensive men in a trapping situation and one defensive man in a chance and safety position. We have one offensive man to pass the ball out of the trap using a lob pass to an offensive man under

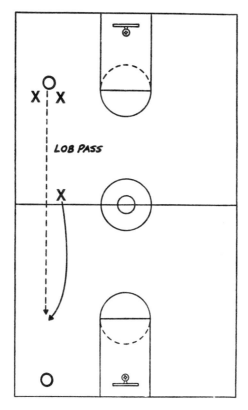

Diagram 3-6

the goal. The chance and safety player sprints on the release of the pass and will intercept the ball or deflect it every time. In most cases, it is too difficult to throw an accurate pass the length of the floor if the proper trapping techniques are used. This will also show the players the importance of a proper trapping technique.

Now that the ball has been trapped and each man assigned to a particular pass interception area (see Diagram 3-5), the ball can only come to one of these men's areas. Only one of our men can intercept the pass; therefore, we want the other four men to get back on defense in case the ball is advanced, to stop the opponents' attack, and to make them set their half court offense up. We back up on the first forward pass after a trap has been made unless we are behind in the late stages of the game. We feel if we are going to press the entire game we can not be giving up the lay-up. By trapping all over the floor, a teams' press becomes more vulnerable to the lay-up. There-

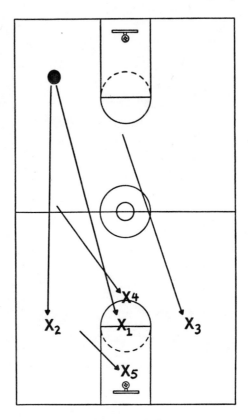

Diagram 3-7

fore, we try to make the offense set up every time if they get by us on the press and we haven't intercepted the ball. With this method you cannot lose by pressing. If we steal the ball ten times a game and convert it and always make them set their offense up if they get the ball up the floor against the press, we feel we have a twenty point advantage on this team from the press alone. It must also be noted that we back up into a zone defense after the ball has been advanced. We do this because it is easier for a player to retreat to a particular spot (this zone area) than it is to find his man. From our 13-1 "Slide and Trap" zone press we will usually back up into a 1-3-1 zone defense. If our scouting report calls for another type of zone, we will use it. Diagram 3-7 illustrates the 1-3-1 regrouping technique when the first forward pass has been made from a double team.

Another pressing technique we spend a lot of time on is teaching our men how to pick up two opponents in an area. This is essential for

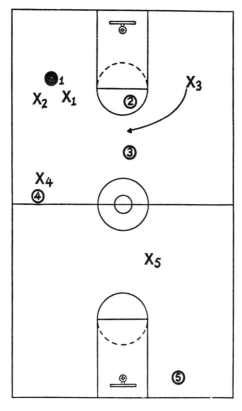

Diagram 3-8

trapping teams. Whenever two pressers trap an opponent, their three teammates are called upon to handle four opponents. That means one of our defenders will have to play two men. Diagram 3-8 illustrates X3 doing this against attackers, 02 and 03. We teach the players to watch the passer's eyes once he has been trapped. Most ball handlers are intimidated when they are trapped and will look right at the player they will throw to. We teach all players to key this and be ready for the pass. This is a technique X3 will use to steal the ball from the attempted pass to the two men in his area.

Diagram 3-9 illustrates the slides and defensive coverages of our 13-1 "Slide and Trap" zone press to the right side. X1, the defensive point man, stays with the inbounds passer until he gets to the free throw line or goes away from the ball (Diagram 3-4) and then traps the opponent with X3, the right wing. X2, the left wing, cuts off the passing lane area around the key. X4, the middle guard, quickly

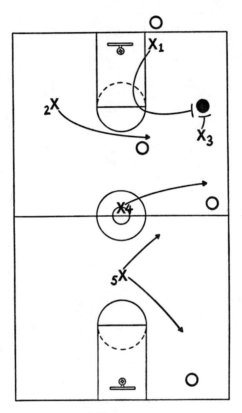

Diagram 3-9

moves over and covers the sideline area to the ball side of the floor.
X5, the chance and safety man, must stop all long lob passes.

    We have mentioned that unless we are behind in the late stages
of the game we back up on the first forward pass after the ball has
been trapped. Therefore, this does not include lateral or backward
passes. We feel on these passes we can keep trapping and not get
hurt. An opponent has ten seconds to cross half court and if we fall
back on lateral passes we cannot get the ball because of the ten second
violation. In any type of zone press the lateral and back area is usually
the most open area so we feel that we *must* trap on these passes.
Diagram 3-10 illustrates the slides we use to trap the ball on a lateral
or back pass from the left side to the right side. Many teams will send
X1 across to double team the ball on a back or lateral pass. It is our
feeling that he cannot see where the ball is being thrown because his
back is turned away from the pass receiver, 02. On lateral or back

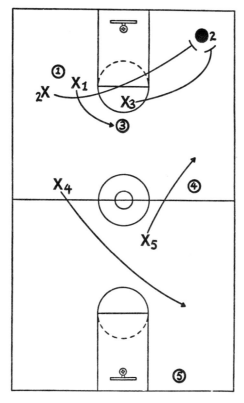

Diagram 3-10

passes from the left to the right side, X1, the defensive point man, will cover the opponent in the area of the key. X2, the left wing, will sprint to the right side and help trap. X3, the right wing, now has trapping responsibility. X4 and X5, now guards, swap assignments on all back or lateral passes. X5, is usually closer to the right sideline and can get to this sideline area quicker than X4, so we give him this sideline responsibility to the ball side of the floor. X4, the middle guard, will drop back and become the chance and safety man on a lateral or back pass.

One of the most important methods of getting the opponent trapped after he has received a lateral or back pass is performed by X3, the right wing. After a lateral pass, many teams will try to get the ball to the middle area as quickly as possible (Diagram 3-11). Most teams complete this pass because many coaches teach the right wing, X3 in Diagram 3-10, to immediately trap the ball when the lateral

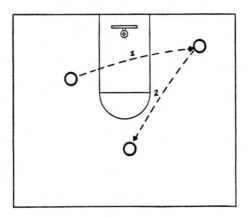

Diagram 3-11

pass is made across court. The method we teach X3 to use is as follows: (See Diagram 3-10.) When the pass is made to 02, hold the opponent in your area, 03, until a count of one-thousand and one. This will give X1 time to get into the key area which is now his responsibility. All passing lanes should now be sealed off and X2 and X3 make the trap. It must also be noted that if 02 puts the ball on the floor seeing that the passing lanes are sealed, X2 must pursue at an angle to trap him and X3 must stop his dribble deeper than usual. This angle pursuit and trap is illustrated in Diagram 3-12.

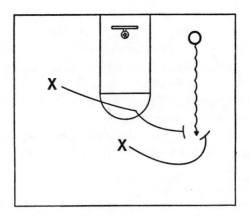

Diagram 3-12

The defensive slides and coverages for lateral and back passes made from the right side to the left side after a trap are illustrated in Diagram 3-13. X1, the defensive point man, seals the passing lane in

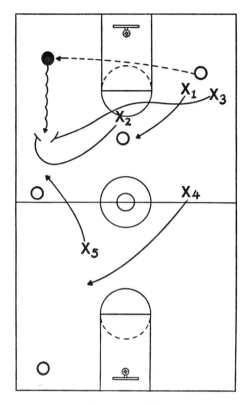

Diagram 3-13

the area of the key. X2, the left wing, nolds the opponent in the key area for a count of one-thousand and one, giving X1 time to pick him up, then laterally slides to trap the ball handler. X3, the right wing, pursues the ball handler and traps with X2. X4, the middle guard, and X5, the chance and safety man, swap assignments. X4 will become the chance and safety man and X5 will assume sideline responsibility to the ball side of the floor.

In the late stages of the game if we are behind, we will use a sideline trap after a forward pass from a trap in back court. Diagram 3-14 illustrates the defensive coverage we use in case the offensive player with the ball is able to complete a pass from the trap to his teammate at the left sideline. X4, the middle guard, upon seeing the opponent receive the pass at the sideline, applies immediate pressure on him and must contain the opponent. X3, the right wing man sprints from the key area in back court to seal off the passing lane near the key area in front court. X2, the left wing, who also was involved in the initial double team, sprints to the mid-court circle and picks up

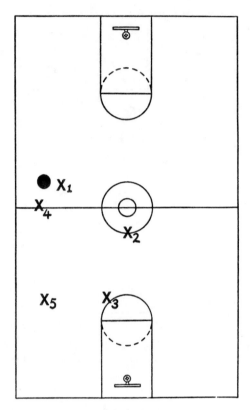

Diagram 3-14

the nearest pass receiver in this area. X5, the chance and safety man, assumes sideline responsibility on the ball side of the floor. X1, the defensive point man, leaves the initial double team and double teams the ball with X4.

If the offensive player with the ball is able to advance the ball from the sideline trap, we will regroup into our pre-designated zone. Diagram 3-15 illustrates our sideline trap coverages after a successful forward pass to the sidelines on the right side of the floor from an initial trap. X1, the defensive point man, and X4, the middle guard, double team the ball at the right sideline near mid-court. X2, the left wing, seals off the passing lane in the area around the key. X3, the right wing, anticipates any pass in the area of the half court circle. X5, the chance and safety man, overplays any opponent at the sideline on the ball side of the floor.

Many times we have faced teams with a super guard and a weak

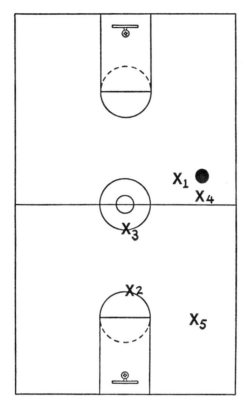

Diagram 3-15

or average guard. A 13-1 "Slide and Trap" stunt we can use in this situation is shown in Diagram 3-16. 01 is the super guard and 02 is the weak or average guard. This stunt is used to keep the ball away from the super player on the inbounds pass. To make sure he does not get the ball, X1, the defensive point man, will front him and X2, the left wing, will play behind him. This seals off the passing lanes. X3, the right wing, is told to let 02 have the ball in. After the pass is made to the weak or average guard, we use our basic zone press principles.

When a team attacks us with a three man front, Diagram 3-17, or a four man front, Diagram 3-18, we can use our 13-1 "Slide and Trap" press.

Initial alignment against a three man offensive attack for the inbounds pass is illustrated in Diagram 3-19. We have moved X1, the defensive point man, off the ball against this set. He must front any man that breaks into the middle and keep him from getting the ball.

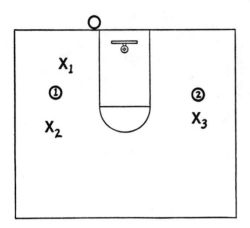

Diagram 3-16

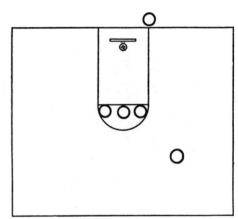

Diagram 3-17

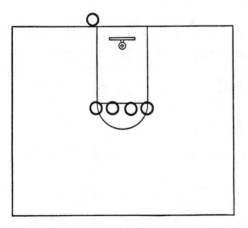

Diagram 3-18

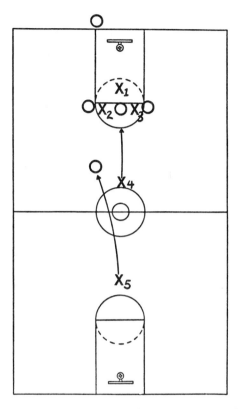

Diagram 3-19

X1 is the only man that will overplay the inbounds pass unless the other players are certain that they can get the ball. Usually a team with a three man offensive attack will keep breaking a different man to the corners for the inbounds pass. Therefore, we tell the wing men, X2 and X3, to think primarily of picking up one of the three men that comes to his area. If we wanted to use a full overplay against this three man attack, we would use our "snipe attack." (Full court man-to-man press with overplay as illustrated in Chapter Two.) The 13-1 "Slide and Trap" defensive slides and coverages are used once the inbounds pass is completed.

A team that attacks with four men on the inbounds pass will again usually break different men to the corners at various times. A four man attack that teams have used and the defensive alignment and coverages we use on the inbounds pass in our 13-1 "Slide and Trap" press are illustrated in Diagram 3-20. X1, the defensive point man,

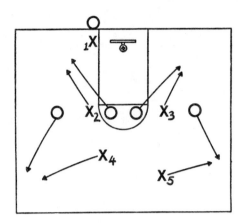

Diagram 3-20

applies pressure on the ball. X2, the left wing, takes the man that breaks to his corner. X3, the right wing, takes the opponent that breaks to the right corner. The wing men can only overplay if they are sure of making the steal. X4, the middle guard, has positioned himself two or three steps above the key shading the left side, and overplays the pass to the opponent that breaks to the left corner. X5, the chance and safety man, is approximately half way between the key area and mid-court shading the right side, and overplays the inbounds pass to the opponent that breaks to the right corner. The 13-1 "Slide and Trap" defensive coverages that were mentioned earlier go into effect after the inbounds pass has been completed.

Our 13-2 "Slide and Trap" press is a 1-2-1-1 full court zone press with full overplay on the inbounds pass. We like to use this press after a successful field goal or free throw. We especially like this press against teams that bring the ball in to one of two primary receivers because we then look like we are in a man-to-man defense. The 13-2 "Slide and Trap" press coverage against a two man offensive attack is shown in Diagram 3-21. We use this press when we are up against teams with average or slow players that are the primary receivers of the inbounds pass. Our personnel positions, do not change; therefore, we still have our forwards at the wing positions, X2 and X3. We can usually only overplay with good risks against the average or slow inbounds receivers. Along with this overplay technique, X1 has a certain responsibility to apply pressure on the inbounds passer for our 13-2 "Slide and Trap" press. He is told to count the five seconds off

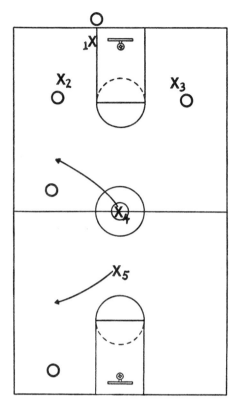

Diagram 3-21

that the inbounds passer has to throw the ball in loudly. Many passers, when hearing the third second called out if they have not passed the ball inbounds, will become intimidated, hurry the pass, and throw the ball away. We tell the defensive point man to start counting the five seconds in a full five seconds count. During the game we tell him to cheat the count (count off the five seconds in less than five seconds) in hopes that the inbounds passer will hurry his pass and throw the ball away. Near the end of a game in which we are behind or need the ball, the defensive point man tries to get to a count of ten within four seconds in hopes that this procedure will cause the inbounds passer to make a bad pass. If the official has heard this high count he may think that the five seconds the passer has to get the pass inbounds has been used up and award us the ball. Many times we have been awarded the ball by the official when using this technique. X2, the left wing, and X3, the right wing, are responsible for overplaying the inbounds pass to their side and must keep their man from getting the ball between the inbounds line and the free throw line. If they execute this properly it will make the inbounds passer throw a long lob pass which the wing man, or the middle guard can intercept. This is shown in Diagram 3-22 using the left side as an example. X4's responsibility on the inbounds pass is to overplay the nearest man in his area (Diagram 3-21) or, as Diagram 3-22 illustrates, pick off the lob passes caused by our wing men. X5, the chance and safety man, is responsible for stopping the long inbounds pass to the man farthest removed from the inbounds passer.

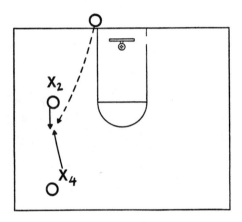

Diagram 3-22

If the inbounds pass is completed in a long lob pass beyond the free throw line, we will back up into a pre-designated zone and will not try to trap the ball. If the inbounds pass is brought in between the free throw line and the inbounds line, we will use the same defensive slides and coverages of our 13-1 "Slide and Trap" press that have been mentioned earlier in the chapter.

THE TROUBLESOME ATTACK
AGAINST THE 1-2-1-1 ZONE PRESS

One of the biggest problems my teams have faced while using the 1-2-1-1 full court zone press is the attack into the middle when the offside offensive guard flashes backdoor toward the front court. This is illustrated in Diagram 3-23. In this attack 01 passes the ball inbounds

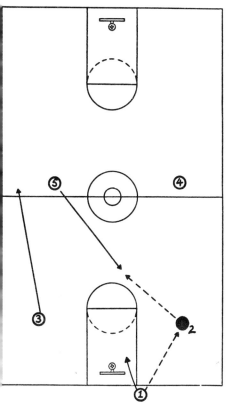

Diagram 3-23

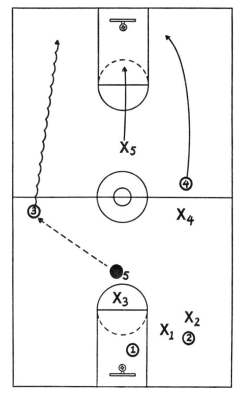

Diagram 3-24

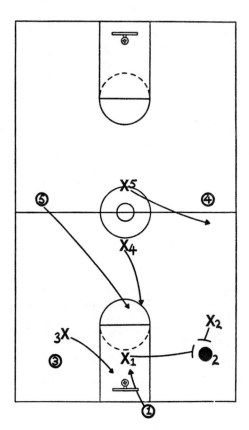

Diagram 3-25

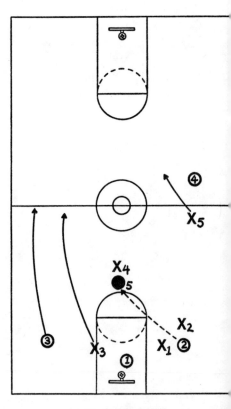

Diagram 3-26

to 02 and steps inbounds for the lateral or back pass. 05 breaks into the middle, receives the ball, and looks backdoor to 03 and passes to him for a two-on-one situation with 04 against X5, (Diagram 3-24). Anytime a team gets this two-on-one situation we feel we are in real trouble.

To defend against this attack we must make an adjustment in our press as shown in Diagram 3-25. In this situation, we have X4, the middle guard, cover the middle area. X5, the chance and safety man, is responsible for the sideline area to the side the ball was brought inbounds to. These two positions are where the adjustments in responsibility are made. X1, the defensive point man, and X2, the left wing, trap the ball after the inbounds pass. X3, the right wing, plays "twixt 'n between" 01 and 03 since they are the two men in his area.

If the pass is completed to 05 into the middle area we have X3, the right wing, chase 03 and try to steal the pass from 05 or get between him and the basket forcing a two-on-two situation rather than a two-on-one situation against X5, the chance and safety man. This technique is illustrated in Diagram 3-26.

Chapter 4
Procedures for the
2-1-2 "Slide and Trap"
Full Court Zone Press

The 2-1-2 full court zone press has averaged forcing approximately twenty turnovers in a four quarter span for my teams in the past. I like this press particularly when I have big, quick guards and a mobile center. In this press the guards and the center do most of the trapping. I also like the change in the position from which the trap is sprung.

One of my teams lost to another team by ten points in their gym. When they came to our gym, we utilized this press as our primary press and beat them by 22 points. The 2-1-2 zone press kept them off balance all night and enabled us to be victorious.

ADVANTAGES OF THE 2-1-2 "SLIDE AND TRAP"
FULL COURT ZONE PRESS

The biggest advantage of our 2-1-2 full court "slide and trap" zone press is that it confuses the opponents. The trap is made by the center who comes from the middle of the floor to double team the ball. This technique is different from our other presses and so keeps the opponents off guard.

The 21-2 zone press also keeps teams from playing a slow, deliberate game; it keeps them moving offensively. It keeps this deliberate offense off pace and makes them play our game—the fast, moving game.

Utilizing the 2-1-2 full court "slide and trap" zone press helps us combat teams that have quick guards who can break traps easily. We keep our quick guards up front to trap and this helps us overcome their tendency of breaking the traps set by our big men in most of our other presses.

I can recall many situations in which our presses were being broken because an opponent's quick guards were breaking traps set by our big men. When we changed to our 21-2 full court zone press with our quick guards up front they hesitated to try and break the trap with the dribble. Therefore, we were able to force the lob pass and come up with steals.

2-1-2 "SLIDE AND TRAP"
FULL COURT ZONE PRESS

We use the 2-1-2 full court zone press against teams that use a 2-1-2 or 2-3 offensive set and try to get the ball to one certain man on the inbounds pass. This enables us to match up on the inbounds pass and look like we are playing man-for-man. We call this press our 21-2 "Slide and Trap" press. Diagram 4-1 illustrates the initial alignment of the 21-2 "Slide and Trap" press. X1 and X2 are our guards. X1, the left guard, is the quickest of the guards and must be drilled to perfection on the trapping techniques. X2, the right guard, is also a trapper and must be a good anticipator of passes because most teams will attack the side of X1 which will make him a stealer in his area. X1 and X2 will initially line up at the corners of the free throw line, find the men in their areas, and prevent the inbounds pass. X3, the middle man, initially lines up approximately half way between the top of the key in back court and the half court circle. He is our center and will slide from this position and trap the ball on the side it is brought in on as quickly as possible. On the inbounds pass, he overplays the nearest man in his area to prevent him from getting the ball. His long arms will induce the lob pass making interceptions more vulnerable. X4, the left forward, will initially line up approximately two to three steps beyond the half court line on the left side. He prevents the nearest nen in his area from receiving the inbounds pass and will be a stealer in trapping situations. X5, the right forward, has this same responsibility and initially lines up two to three steps beyond half court to the right side of the floor.

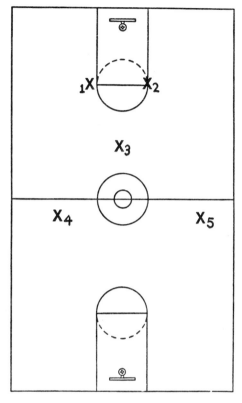

Diagram 4-1

Diagram 4-2 is an illustration of how we will match up for the inbounds pass making us look like we are in a man-to-man defense. In our 21-2 "Slide and Trap" press, you can see that all players overplay the men nearest their areas on the inbounds pass. On all passes completed beyond the free throw line we will back up into a pre-designated zone and will not trap the ball.

Diagram 4-3 shows our defensive slides and coverages against the 2-1-2 offensive set if the ball is not stolen on the inbounds pass and is brought in on the left side between the inbounds line and the free throw line extended. We want X1, the left guard, on the inside shoulder of the ball handler forcing him to the sideline. Every player stays matched up until the ball handler puts the ball on the floor. X3, the middle man, then slides to the sideline and traps with X1. X4, the left forward, has side line responsibility to the ball side of the floor and overplays the man in this area. X5, the right forward, becomes a

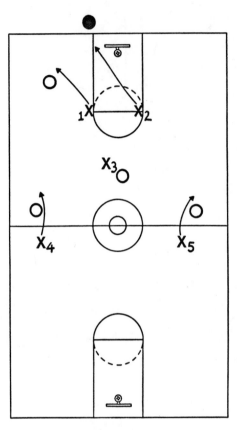

Diagram 4-2

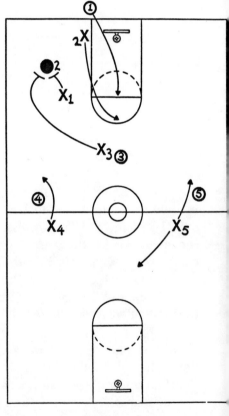

Diagram 4-3

chance and safety man. He can free lance to intercept a pass but is also responsible for protecting the goal area and long passes made to here from the trap. X2, the right guard, is usually the key to this press when the ball is trapped on the left side of the floor. We have found that he is the man that usually has two men in his area so he must play between them and watch the trapped opponent's eyes hoping he will give away who he is going to throw to. Diagram 4-4 shows X2's "twixt and between" technique.

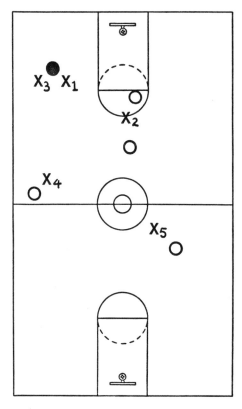

Diagram 4-4
X2 "twixt and between"

In the 21-2 "Slide and Trap" press we will usually regroup into a 2-1-2 zone defense after the first forward pass from back court if it is not intercepted. The identical numbers of the press and the zone makes the regrouping method easier for the players to remember what zone to back up into after the press is broken.

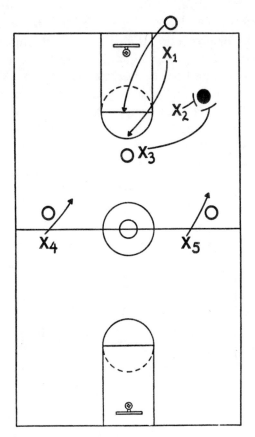

Diagram 4-5

The defensive coverages when the ball is brought in on the right side of the floor between the inbounds line and the free throw line extended are shown in Diagram 4-5. X2, the right guard, forces the ball to the sidelines for the trap with X3, the middle man. X5, the right forward, overplays the opponent on the ball side of the floor looking for the interception. X4, the left forward, is a chance and safety man. X1, the left guard, now has the responsibility of covering two men in his area and plays "twixt and between" them looking for the most likely receiver.

We have mentioned that we like a sideline trap from this press. However, when using a two guard front, a team will get the inbounds pass in the middle area around the free throw lane. When this occurs we use a "middle area trap." This technique is illustrated in Diagram 4-6 showing an inbounds pass on the right side to this middle area.

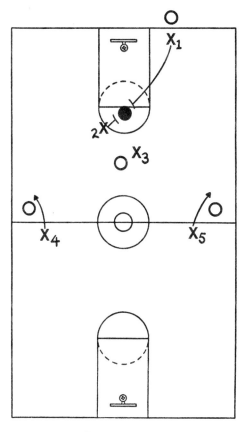

Diagram 4-6

X2, the right guard, must contain the ball handler so X1, the left guard, will be able to help trap. X3, the middle man, X4, the left forward, and X5, the right forward, stay matched up with the men in their areas and prevent them from getting the pass. The defensive man whose area the inbounds passer comes to must be ready to play between two opponents and watch the passer's eyes in hopes he will give away whom he is going to throw to so the steal can be made. If the ball handler takes more than three dribbles and is not trapped, X3, X4, and X5 regroup into their half court zone area while X1, and X2 try to stop the ball handler's advancement. Once they can make him give up his dribble, X1 will keep pressure on him and X2 will drop back into the standard zone defense.

The middle area trap from an inbounds pass on the left side to the middle area around the free throw lane is shown in Diagram 4-7.

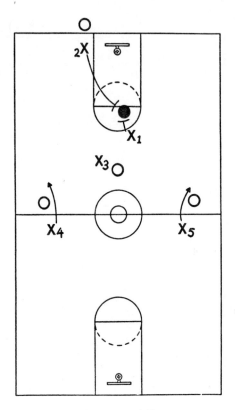

Diagram 4-7

X3, X4 and X5's assignments and techniques remain the same on all middle area traps. X1 must contain the ball handler so X2 will be able to trap.

All lateral or back passes are treated the same as the inbounds passes completed between the inbounds line and the free throw line extended. These defensive slides and coverages are shown in Diagrams 4-3 and 4-5.

The sideline trap we use from our 21-2 "Slide and Trap" press on the left side when we are behind or in desperate need of the ball is shown in Diagram 4-8. X4, the left forward, upon seeing the pass completed from the initial trap to the man in his area, contains the ball handler. X3, the middle man, leaves the initial trap and sprints to the ball handler to trap with X4. X1, the left guard, releases from the initial trap and sprints to the half court circle and looks to intercept the ball in this area. X2, the right guard, leaves the key area in back court and anticipates passes in the key area in the front court. X5, the right forward, assumes sideline responsibility on the ball side of the floor.

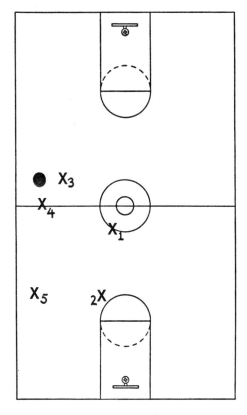

Diagram 4-8

A slide and trap stunt we use with our 21-1 press is illustrated in Diagram 4-9. We use this stunt when there are fewer than five seconds to play in a quarter or when we are behind and must have the ball. As soon as we score, X1, the left guard, and X2, the right guard double team the inbounds passer. X3, the middle man, covers the near inbounds receiver. X4, the left forward, covers the sideline area to the ball side of the floor. X5, the right forward, who has two men in his area will play between and try to intercept any pass in the key area.

DEFENSING THROW-INS ON DIFFERENT AREAS OF THE COURT

Several times during a game the team that is pressing will hit the ball out of bounds while attempting to make a steal. This brings about

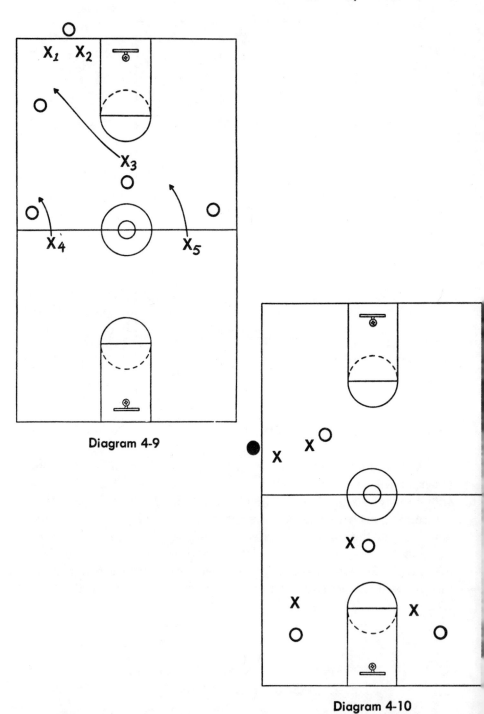

Diagram 4-9

Diagram 4-10

the sideline throw-in by the opponent. In all instances except when we are using the 21-2 full court zone press, we automatically play a man-to-man defense on a thrown-in, Diagram 4-10.

But when we are using the 21-2 full court zone press, we back up into a 1-2-2 zone on a throw-in. We have been regrouping into a 2-1-2 zone with this press and the 1-2-2 defensive set in the front court is a different look and provides us with another defensive variation. A coach can create these pressing variations in all sideline throw-in situations if he desires. Basically, I like to use the man-to-man defense on sideline throw-ins, but to add a little kink in our pressing variations, we use the 1-2-2 defensive set and trap the ball as it crosses the half court line. This technique is illustrated in Diagram 4-11 with the ball being brought across half court on the right side. We set up just as we do in the standard 1-2-2 zone defense. Nobody moves until the ball is dribbled across the half court line into the front court.

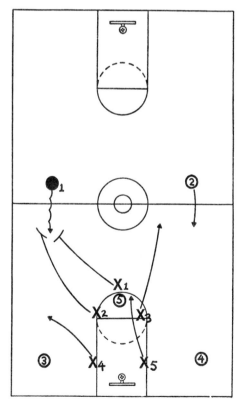

Diagram 4-11

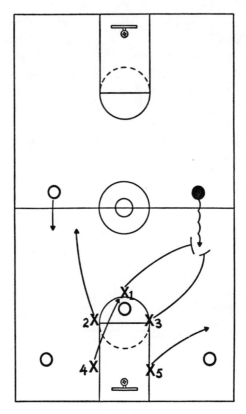

Diagram 4-12

When this happens, everybody moves at once. X1 and X2 double team the dribbler, 01. X3 will defend the lateral pass which is to the other guard, 02. X4 is responsible for stopping the sideline pass, which, in this case, is to 03. X5 is responsible for cutting off the pass into the middle area, which is 05 in this situation. If the ball is brought down the left side of the floor (Diagram 4-12), X1 and X3 double team the dribbler. X5 is responsible for the sideline area. X4 cuts off the middle area near the high post. X2 stops the lateral pass to the other guard.

If a pass is completed to any opponent, we automatically regroup into our 1-2-2 standard zone defense. This regrouping must be done quickly because we are vulnerable to lay-ups if we do not.

Chapter 5
Ways to Use the 2-2-1
"Slide and Trap"
Full Court Zone Press

The 2-2-1 full court zone press is another "Slide and Trap" press we use in our system. We call this press our 22-2 "Slide and Trap" zone press.

The 2-2-1 zone press has been a very effective press for us during the past few years. One of the fondest memories I have of this press is when I saw its use bring one of my teams from a 13-4 deficit in the early moments of a game to an eight point victory. The opponent had the momentum early, but the 2-2-1 zone press stopped this momentum and transferred it to our hands.

ADVANTAGES OF THE 2-2-1 "SLIDE AND TRAP"
FULL COURT ZONE PRESS

Our players like a press that is working. For example, if we are using our 13-1 zone press and it is not working, we need a zone press variation. The 2-2-1 full court zone press has been great for a change of pace and against teams that attack us with a 2-2-1 offensive set.

When we change into our 2-2-1 full court zone press and it starts working, the attitude of the team both on the floor and on the bench becomes positive. This positive attitude helps us offensively as well as defensively. It builds confidence. We have found that our players begin to shoot, pass, dribble, fast break, and run patterns better

because of a positive attitude that has resulted from baffling opponents with the 2-2-1 full court zone press.

THE 2-2-1 "SLIDE AND TRAP" FULL COURT ZONE PRESS

The 2-2-1 full court zone press is another "Slide and Trap" press
we use in our system. We call this press our 22-2 "Slide and Trap"
zone press. We use this 22-2 "Slide and Trap" press mostly against
teams that attack us with a 2-2-1 offensive set which makes it easier for
us to match up on the inbounds pass and look like we are in a man-
to-man defense.

Many teams will start out attacking us with a 2-3 set and after we
have caused them to turn the ball over drop a man deep from this set
causing a 2-2-1 offensive look. This is illustrated in Diagram 5-1. Of

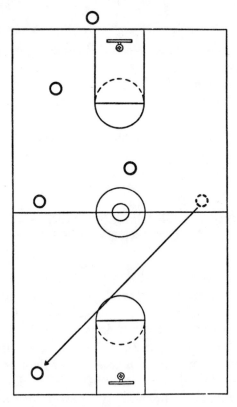

Diagram 5-1

course many teams will start out in this set. If this shift is being made, the floor captain will call out the audible 22-2 telling our players to go into this "Slide and Trap" press.

When using the 22-2 press and all other full court zone presses, quick transition from offense to defense is a must. The best method of beating the full court zone press is getting the ball on the inbounds pass in so fast that the defensive team cannot get their press set up. Therefore, we tell our players that as soon as we have scored, they must set up defensively within three seconds although we feel four to four and one-half seconds is usually sufficient time. We time our players on this transition during our practice sessions to perfect this.

The initial floor alignment that the players use to find their man and match up for the inbounds pass is shown in Diagram 5-2. X1, the left guard, and X2, the right guard, initially line up at the corners of the free throw lane. They will be trappers to their respective side and

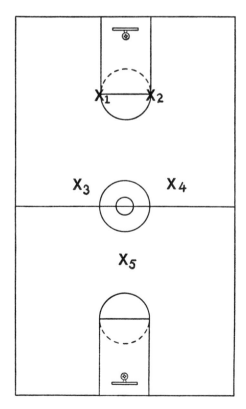

Diagram 5-2

a stealer when the ball is away from them. They will also prevent inbounds passes by using overplay techniques. The guard techniques in our 22-2 press are the same on the inbounds pass as the 21-2 press. X3, the left forward, lines up to the left side approximately six to eight feet above the half court line. X4, the right forward, lines up to the right side approximately six to eight feet above the half court line. X5 is the safety man on the inbounds pass and lines up approximately three feet below the half court circle to stop the long passes.

Diagram 5-3 illustrates the basic defensive coverages we use against the 2-2-1 offensive set to stop the inbounds pass on the 22-2 "Slide and Trap" press when the ball is attempted to be brought in on the left side. As you can see, the guard technique is the same as our 21-2 "Slide and Trap" press. X2, the right guard, pressures the inbounds passer. X1, the left guard, overplays the primary receiver and does not allow him to get the ball. X3, the left forward, overplays the

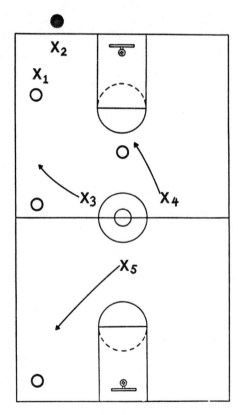

Diagram 5-3

man in the sideline area. X4, the right forward, takes the nearest man in his area and prevents him from getting the inbounds pass. X5, the chance and safety man, prevents the long inbounds pass to the deep man.

Diagram 5-4 shows the defensive coverages for the inbounds pass in our 22-2 "Slide and Trap" press when the ball is being brought in on the right side. X1, the left guard, pressures the passer as X2 fronts the primary receiver. X3, the left forward, covers the near man who is in the area around the key. X4, the right forward, assumes sideline responsibility. X5, the chance and safety man, prevents the long bomb.

If the inbounds pass is completed beyond the free throw line extended, we will regroup into our pre-designated zone, which is usually a 1-2-2 zone with this press. If the ball is brought in success- fully between the free throw line extended and the inbounds line, we

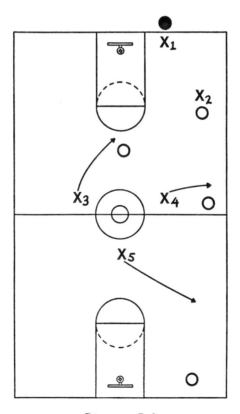

Diagram 5-4

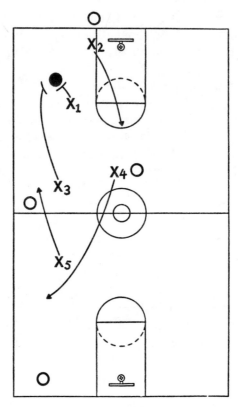

Diagram 5-5

will trap. Diagram 5-5 illustrates the basic defensive slides and coverages we use when trapping the ball to the left side in our 22-2 press. It
must be noted that quick shifts in this press, as in all presses, are very
important. We tell all defensive players but X3 they *must shift to their
areas as soon as the ball leaves the inbounds passer's fingertips and
positively no later.* We will practice on this shift every day until we
get it down. X3, the left forward, in an effort to make the ball handler
put the ball on the floor, will count one thousand and one before he
moves in to trap. We hope that this will cause the opponent to start
his dribble then pick it up, taking away one of the two threats he has
(passing or dribbling). This hesitation will also give X5 more time to
shift to the sideline area. X1, the left guard, seeing that he cannot
steal the inbounds pass will force the opponent to the sideline by
overplaying his inside shoulder. X2, the right guard, seeing the ball
leave the inbounds passer's fingertips quickly shifts to stop the quick

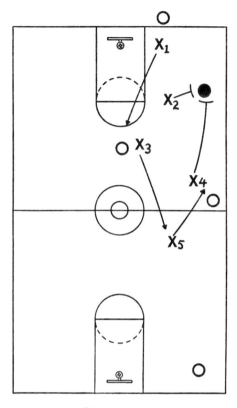

Diagram 5-6

return pass in the middle area. The middle area is the weak spot in this press and X2 must stop this vulnerability. X3, the left forward, holds for one second and traps with X1. X4, the right forward, becomes the chance and safety man when the ball is to the left side of the floor. X5, the safety man on the inbounds pass, overplays the passing lane on the ball side of the floor.

Diagram 5-6 illustrates the slides and coverages we use to the right side after a successful inbounds pass between the free throw line extended and the inbounds line. X2, the right guard, and X4, the right forward, trap the ball handler. X1, the left guard, cuts off the passing lanes in the middle area. X3, the left forward, becomes a chance and safety man. X5, the right forward, assumes sideline responsibility of the ball side of the floor.

In the 22-1 "Slide and Trap" press we will use a sideline trap when we are behind or in desperate need of the ball. The sideline

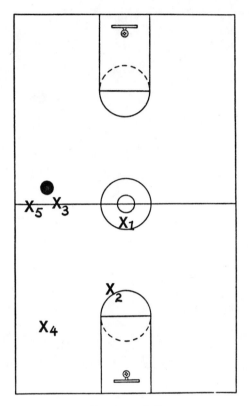

Diagram 5-7

trap from this press on the left side of the floor after a forward pass is completed is illustrated in Diagram 5-7. X5, safety man, who had sideline responsibility, seeing the forward pass completed must contain the opponent so X3, the left forward, can leave the initial trap and double team with him. X1, the left guard, sprints to cover the area around the half court. X2, the right guard, leaves the area around the key in back court and sprints to cut off passes to the key area in the front court. X4, the right forward, cuts off the sideline pass on the left side. We have found this sideline trap to be very effective because X1 and X2, our guards, have the farthest route to travel but can get there quicker than anybody else could because of their speed. This method allows the passing lanes to be cut off quicker. Our big men are again trapping which we feel will induce the lob pass or intimidate the ball handler more.

The defensive slides and coverages of the sideline trap on the

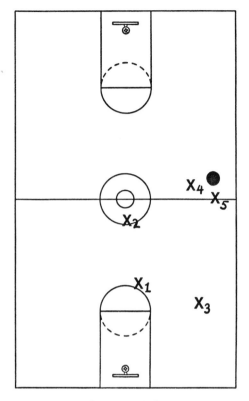

Diagram 5-8

right side of the floor are shown in Diagram 5-8. X4, the right forward, and X5, the safety man on the inbounds pass, trap the opponent
at the sideline area near mid-court. X2, the right guard, leaves the
back court trap and anticipates the pass around half court. X1, the left
guard, sprints from back court to anticipate passes near the key area
in front court. X3, the left forward, assumes sideline responsibility on
the right side.

    In our 22-1 "Slide and Trap" press, all lateral and back pass
coverages are treated the same as the coverages on the inbounds
passes (Diagrams 5-5 and 5-6).

    If a team gets the ball in the middle area near the free throw line
on the inbounds pass from the left side, we use the defensive coverages illustrated in Diagram 5-9. X1, the left guard, must contain the
opponent as X2, the right guard, retreats to converge with him for
the double team. X3, the left defensive forward, X4, the defensive

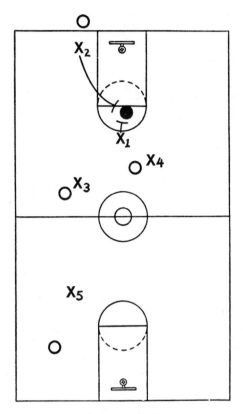

Diagram 5-9

right forward, and X5, the safety man, stay matched up with the men in their areas and cut off the passing lanes. The man whose area the inbounds passer comes to must be ready to play the two men in his area "twixt and between." If the ball handler takes more than three dribbles and is not trapped X3, X4 and X5, back up into their half court zone, while X1, and X2 try to stop the opponent from advancing the ball. Once they stop him X1 will keep applying pressure on him while X2 retreats to his zone area.

The middle area trap from an inbounds pass on the right side is shown in Diagram 5-10. X1 and X2, the guards, double team the ball while X3 and X4, the forwards match up with the nearest man in their area. X5, the safety man, prevents the long pass to the back man. On the back-up rule after three dribbles, X2 and X1 will stop the dribbler's advancement, and once they do this X2 will keep applying

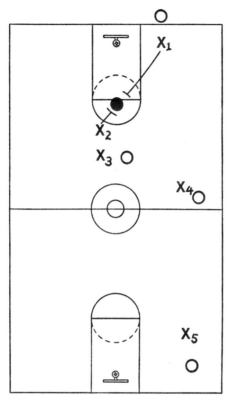

Diagram 5-10

pressure to him while X1 regroups into a zone with X3, X4 and X5 who regrouped after the dribbler took more than three dribbles.

We have a stunting technique in our 22·2 "Slide and Trap" press for teams who have a fantastic player they want to get the inbounds pass to. The stunt is to prevent them from getting the ball to this player on the inbounds pass. We will also use this stunt in the late stages of the game when we are in desperate need of the ball. Diagram 5-11 illustrates this stunt from our 22-2 press. 02 is the fantastic ball player so we will remove X2, the right guard, off the inbounds passer and have him front 02. X1, the left guard, will play behind 02. This should cut the pass off to this primary receiver. X3, the left forward, X4, the right forward, and X5, the safety man, overplay the man in their areas on the inbounds pass looking for the steal. As you can see we have created a five on four situation—not bad odds!

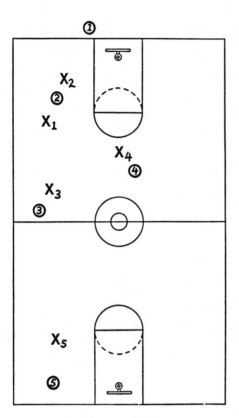

Diagram 5-11

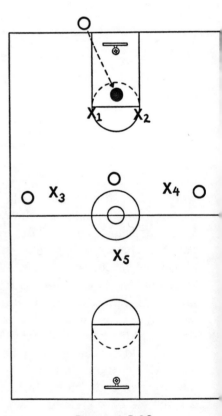

Diagram 5-12

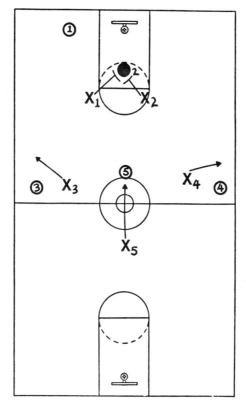

Diagram 5-13

DEFENSING THROW-INS TO THE MIDDLE AREA

When using the 2-2-1 full court zone press, it is almost inevitable that opponents will make their inbounds pass to the middle area of the floor near the free throw line (Diagram 5-12). When this occurs we want X1 and X2 to apply extreme pressure on the ball; X3 and X4 should seal off the passing lanes at their respective sideline areas; and X5 should seal off the middle passing lane. This is illustrated in Diagram 5-13.

The key to this defensive situation is that this technique will force the ball handler 02, to pass the ball to 01 the inbounds passer. Now the ball is at the side of the court where we can use our regular trapping stunts from our 22-1 "slide and trap" press (Diagram 5-14). X1 the defensive left guard, releases from the double team and forces 01 into a double team with X3, the defensive left forward. X2, the

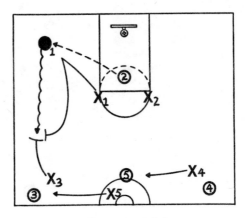

Diagram 5-14

defensive right guard, stops the pass back to 02 near the foul line. X5, the chance and safety man, will overplay the passing lane to 03 on the ball side of the floor. X4, the defensive right forward, will stop the pass to the farthest receivers, 04 or 05.

Chapter 6
Methods for Using the Three-Quarter Court "Dogging" Presses

The three-quarter court zone press has proven to be a winner for my ball clubs. It is a very good, conservative press in that the gambles taken are not as great as the full court.

During one season I can remember being behind twelve points in the first quarter of a game. We had been employing the full court zone press. The team we were playing was much quicker than we were, and they were getting the ball inbounds so fast that we did not have the time to set up our full court zone press. Backing our press up to the three-quarter court level allowed us the opportunity to set up our press and attack this quicker team. We ended up winning the game by eight points and it was because of our three-quarter court pressing techniques. We caused this team to make approximately twenty-eight turnovers by the end of the game.

We use the three-quarter court zone press after a successful field goal or free throw. The three-quarter court zone presses we use are called our "dogging" presses. We use this term to instill in our players that we want them to get after the opponents like a hungry dog would go after his bone. The three-quarter court zone presses we use are the 1-2-1-1; 2-1-2; and the 2-2-1. We call the 1-2-1-1 three-quarter court zone press our "Mad-dog" press. Our 2-1-2 three-quarter court zone press is called our "Bulldog" press. The 2-2-1 three-quarter court zone press is our "Boxer" press. We change our presses a lot and when our floor captain yells out one of these names our players easily know what three-quarter technique to go into.

ADVANTAGES

When using multiple presses as we do, we might use the same alignment as in our full court or half court zone presses, but the personnel look is different, thereby causing confusion to the opponent. For example, we use a 1-2-1-1 alignment in both the full court and three-quarter court zone presses. The differences between these presses is in the placement of the personnel. In the 1-2-1-1 full court zone press, our big man plays up front and our guards in the back, but in our 1-2-1-1 three-quarter court zone press, our guards are up front and the big man is in the back. Creating a different "look" by changing from full court to three-quarter court zone press will sometimes baffle a team as it comes down the floor.

The three-quarter court zone press is a great press for the team which does not have much depth. A team with no depth can not afford to use the full court press the whole game because the gamble is too great. When pressing all over the floor players will foul more and when a coach has no bench to replace people that foul out he is going to be in trouble. I have seen many coaches lose basketball games because they utilized the full court press the entire game and when the fourth quarter started, they only had two or three starters on the floor. Also when a team likes to press but has no depth, conditioning becomes a big factor. Using the full court zone press an entire game is very, very demanding. A team can completely give out when using the full court zone press if there is no bench to back them up. Thus, by using the three-quarter court press a pressing team with no depth will find it less demanding physically and will also find that the gambles are not as great.

The three-quarter court press prevents a team from holding the ball on us. When we apply the three-quarter court zone press we make the opponent attack our defense and not allow him to hold the ball.

The three-quarter court zone press allows a team to take advantage of the opponent that has poor passing ability. When using the three-quarter court zone press, it is hoped that the ball will be trapped every time near the hash mark in back court causing a double team situation on the ball. The opponent has only one alternative when he is trapped at three-quarter court and that is to pass. Therefore, we are taking advantage of his weakness which is passing.

1-2-1-1 THREE-QUARTER "MAD-DOG" ZONE PRESS

This is the first zone press that I taught. We give it the name "Mad-dog" because we want our players to press opponents as a mad dog would. We use this press most of the time after a successful free throw. Also, if the scouting report shows that a team is weak against this press, we will use it as our primary press for the game.

The initial alignment of our 1-2-1-1 three-quarter "Mad-dog" zone press is shown in Diagram 6-1.

X1, the point man, is our biggest guard. He lines up at the free throw line in the back court and forces the dribbler down the right or left sideline from the inbounds pass. He is one of the trappers and must be drilled constantly on the techniques of trapping. When trap-

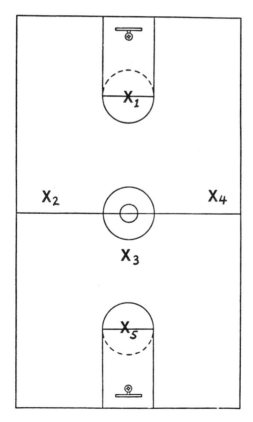

Diagram 6-1

ping the ball, he should try to force the lob pass for an interception or a bad pass for a turnover.

X2, the left wing, is one of our forwards and lines up two or three steps above the half court line on the left side. We put our best defensive forward at this position because most teams will attack to his side. This is because most dribblers are right-handed and will come this way. He is one of our trappers when the ball comes down on his side and must also be drilled on the trapping techniques. It is hoped that his long arms will again induce the lob pass.

X4, the right wing, is usually a forward and lines up two or three steps above the half court line on the right side. He must be able to trap the ball when it comes to his side. He should also be able to intercept passes when the ball is trapped on X2's side.

X3, the middle guard, is our quickest man. He initially lines up two or three steps below the half court line. He is known as the interceptor because he usually gets most of the steals. He must be the best anticipator of passes.

X5, the safety man, is our big man and sets up at the free throw line in the front court. We place him back to reject shots when a team breaks our press. Many times teams will break our press and have a two-on-one situation but we use our "moose" to intimidate and force a blocked shot, a bad shot, or a bad pass. After a team makes these mistakes a few times, we have found that when they break the press again they are content to set the ball up. This is a great advantage for us because we have time to retreat to our standard defense.

Diagram 6-2 illustrates the slides and defensive coverages of our "mad-dog" press to the right side. X1, the defensive point man, forces the dribbler down the sideline into a trap with X2, our left wing. It is X1's responsibility to keep the opponent with the basketball from going between X1 and X2's trap (Diagram 6-3) and it is X2's responsibility to keep the ball handler from going between him and the sideline (Diagram 6-4). Timing is very important when trapping, and it is only through practice that a team can get this timing down. I have known many coaches who unsuccessfully pressed because they did not work on trapping. It is a must and is the key to all presses. If there is no trap or double team, a basketball team will not have a very good press. A coach can not expect to work on trapping six or seven times a year and have a good group of trappers. He must work almost every day on it. Before the season starts, a team must work long and hard on trapping techniques. Once the season starts, the team needs only five

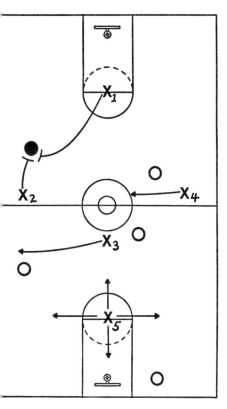

Diagram 6-2

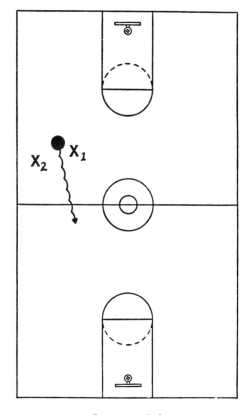

Diagram 6-3

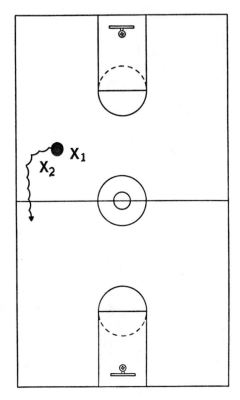

Diagram 6-4

or six minutes a day on it, but the coach must utilize these few minutes each practice day for an efficient trapping press.

X3, the middle guard, will always be responsible for cutting off the passes to the sideline. He is the quickest guard and can cover all of the sideline territories. It must also be noted that if there is not anyone in his area, he picks up the man nearest to his area. Diagram 6-5 is an illustration of this. A team will find this situation when an opposing team is clearing out for a player.

X4, the right wing, is an interceptor when the ball is trapped on the right side. He has the responsibility of stopping passes to the middle area and usually is the man who has two opponents in his area. He must play in between these players so that he can pick off the pass to either player. (This technique is shown in Diagram 3-8.)

X5, the safety man, protects the basket and waylays all long passes around the lane area. He is told that he can go after the ball outside this area anytime but he had better come up with the basketball!

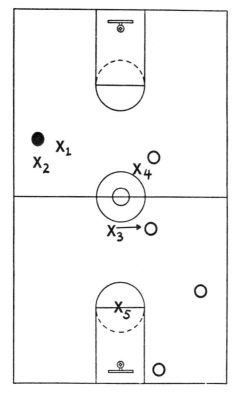

Diagram 6-5

It must be noted that we always retreat to our standard defense (usually a zone after the press) when the first forward pass is made or when the ball is dribbled across the half court line. These are our two retreating rules for all of our three-quarter court presses.

In our three-quarter court presses we do not retreat on lateral or back passes because we want to get the ball from the ten second violation or from a bad pass caused by trapping the ball on the other side. Diagram 6-6 illustrates the slides and coverages we use on a lateral or back pass in our "mad-dog" press when the ball is passed from the right side to the left side. X2, the left wing, is in a better position to see the pass to the left side from the trap than X1, the defensive point man. Therefore, we will send X2 to the left side to trap with X4, the right wing, who leaves the middle area to trap the ball. X3, the middle guard, again has sideline responsibility. We send him to the sideline instead of X5 because we do not want our big man away from the basket if our opponents do break the press and cause a

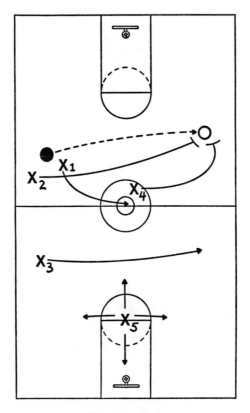

Diagram 6-6

two-on-one or three-on-one sitation. X5, the safety man, again must protect the basket.

The defensive slides and coverages when the ball is brought up on the left side is shown in Diagram 6-7. X1, the defensive point man, and X4, the right wing, will be our trappers. X4 must not let the dribbler break the press by going between him and the sideline, and X1 must not let the opponent dribble through the trap between him and X4. X3, the middle guard, has sideline responsibility. X5, the safety man, protects the basket area. X2, the left wing, has middle area coverage.

Diagram 6-8 shows the shifts made on a lateral or back pass from the left side trap to the right side. X4, the right wing, and X2, the left wing, will trap the ball. X3, the middle guard, has sideline responsibility. X1, the defensive point man, covers the middle area. X5, the safety man, protects the basket.

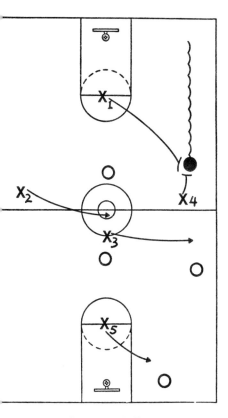

Diagram 6-7

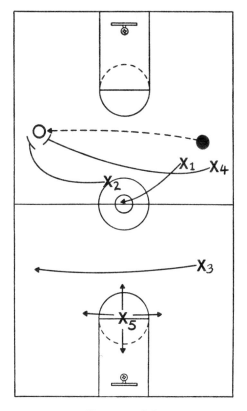

Diagram 6-8

Our standard regrouping defense from our "mad-dog" press is the 1-3-1 zone defense. We retreat to this defense when the opponent completes the first forward pass or when the ball is dribbled across half court. Once again if they break our zone press, we make them attack our 1-3-1 zone defense. Thus, they must combat two defenses—the "mad-dog" press and the 1-3-1 zone. The regrouping technique from the right side of the floor is shown in Diagram 6-9. As you can see, the 1-3-1 zone provides our players with an easy method of retreating. X1, the defensive point man and one of our guards, will now play the point in the 1-3-1 zone. X2, the left wing and one of the forwards, plays the left wing in the zone. X4, the right wing and a forward, now has the responsibility of playing the right wing in the 1-3-1 zone. X3, the middle guard, plays the baseline in the zone. X5, the safety man and our center, plays the center position in the 1-3-1 zone.

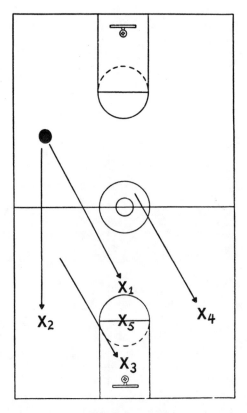

Diagram 6-9

Diagram 6-10 shows the regrouping method from the left side. X1 retreats to the defensive point position, X4 regroups to the right wing position, X2 backs up to cover the left wing, X3 plays the baseline position, and X5 plays the middle position in the 1-3-1 zone.

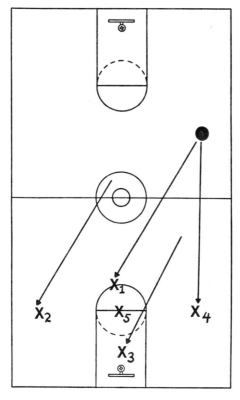

Diagram 6-10

THE 2-1-2 THREE-QUARTER "BULLDOG" PRESS

When the floor captain calls out the word "bulldog" on the floor or if I tell my team we are going to use the bulldog press, we use a 2-1-2 three-quarter court press against our opponent. We like to use this as a change-of-pace when we are using the three-quarter court press as a primary press. Doing this frequently causes a team to panic because it gives us a new look with our three-quarter zone presses. We also use this press against teams whose quickness makes it dif-

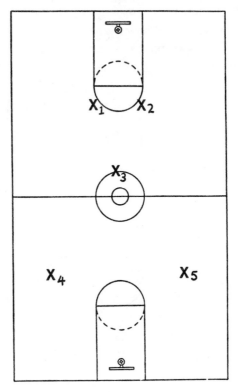

Diagram 6-11

ficult for us to use a full court zone press and who attack us with a 2-1-2 offensive set. This allows us to match-up with them and cause more confusion. Diagram 6-11 illustrates the initial alignment of our 2-1-2 three-quarter "bulldog" press. X1 and X2 are both guards. X1, the left guard, is a drilled trapper and lines up on the left side at the top of the key in back court. We put our best trapping guard on this side because most teams will bring the ball up his side. X2, the right guard, is also a trapper and lines up on the right side of the key in the back court. X3, the middle man, initially lines up at the top of the circle at half court. X3 is our center and traps the ball on the sideline up which the opponent brings the ball. We want his long arms in this trapping situation to promote the lob pass by the opponent. X4 and X5 are our forwards. X4, the left forward, initially lines up on the left side approximately seven feet from the twenty-seven foot hash mark in the front court. X5, the right forward, assumes this same positioning on the right side of the floor.

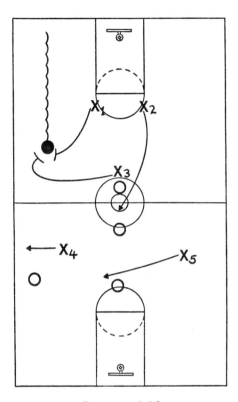

Diagram 6-12

In the "bulldog" press we allow the opponents to bring the ball in. Our guards always force the ball to the sideline and must not let the ball come up the middle. It is the guard's job to turn the basketball to the sideline if the ball is on his side. The slides and coverages we use when the ball is brought to the right side are shown in Diagram 6-12. X1, the left guard, must force the ball to the sideline to trap with X3. X3, the middle man, laterally slides to his left and traps the basketball with X1. X3's timing and maneuvers are very important. He is taught not to be waiting for the dribbler but rather to laterally slide a step for each dribble. What he is doing is sneaking up on the dribbler. Timing is important in this maneuver and it is only through practice that he can learn to accomplish this. X2, the right guard, is also a trapper but must be an interceptor when the ball comes up the right side of the floor. His responsibility is to cover opponents in the area of the half court circle and anticipate the pass. Ninety per cent of the time he will have two men in his area and he

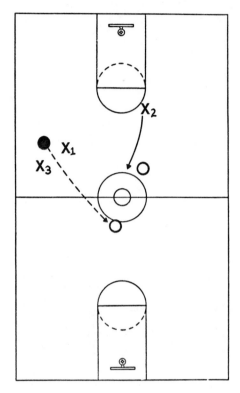

Diagram 6-13

must play between both of the opponents, watch the passer's eyes and get the steal if the ball is thrown to either of the two players in his area. He cannot play one of the players tight and leave a player in his area open as shown in Diagram 6-13. X4, the left forward, has the responsibility of cutting off all the passes to the sidelines area. He also cannot play his man too tight or the passer will not throw the ball into his area. He must play just loose enough to let the passer think he has an open man at the sideline area, and then when the opponent does pass into this area, he goes for the interception. X5, the right forward, has the responsibility of covering men in the area of the key in the front court. When the successful trap is made in our bulldog press, we should have formed a cup around the basketball and should be able to intercept any forward pass that is attempted (Diagram 6-14).

When we are using the "bulldog" press, we use a stunt that has proven to be very effective for us, especially towards the middle or end of the game (Diagram 6-15). Instead of having X3, the middle

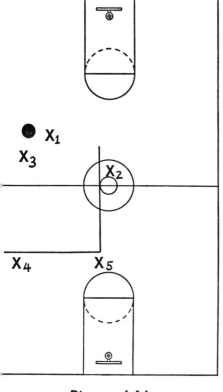

Diagram 6-14

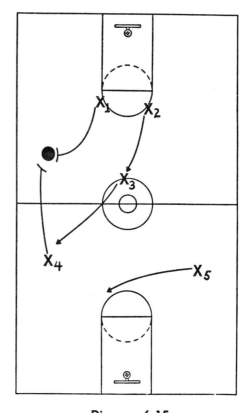

Diagram 6-15

man, trap the ball with X1, the left guard, we stunt with X4, the left forward. We send him to trap the ball with X1 and have X3 assume sideline responsibility. All we have done is swapped X1's and X3's assignments. All other assignments remain the same. This stunting has confused our opponents many times. Anytime we press, we have found that the more stunts we can use the more effective our press will be.

The defensive slides and coverages we use when the ball is brought inbounds on the left side are illustrated in Diagram 6-16. These are also the same slides we use on all back or lateral passes from the right side to the left side. As you can see, assignments in this press are very simple. X2, the right guard, forces the ball to the sideline to trap the ball with X3, the middle man. X1, the left guard, is responsible for any men near the half court circle. He will usually have two men in his area and must play "twixt and between" them. X5, the

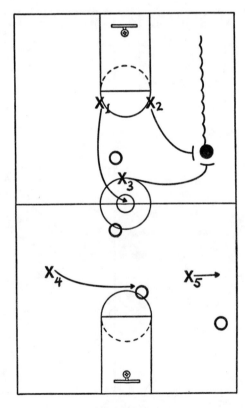

Diagram 6-16

right forward, has the responsibility of covering the sideline area on the side of the ball. X4, the left forward, is responsible for the area around the top of the key in the front court.

When we stunt to this side, Diagram 6-17, we swap X3's and X5's assignments giving us a different look with the press. X2, the right guard, and X5, the right forward, trap the dribbler. X3, the middle man who is usually a trapper, covers the sideline area. X1, the left guard, stops passes near the half court circle, and X4, the left forward, rejects passes near the key area in front court.

In our "bulldog" press we regroup into a 2-1-2 zone defense when the first forward pass is completed or when the ball crosses the half court line on the dribble. We feel that since we are in a 2-1-2 three-quarter alignment, it is easier for our players to remember to back up into a 2-1-2 zone defense. The less our players are confused, the better the results. An example of our regrouping technique is

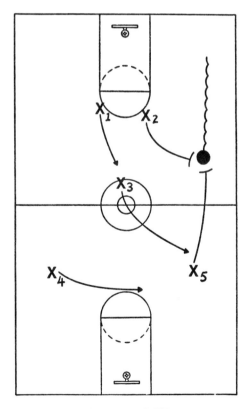

Diagram 6-17

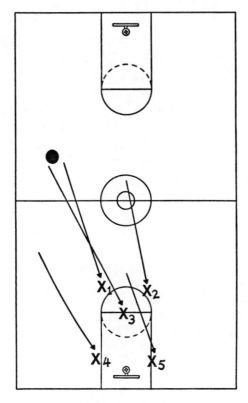

Diagram 6-18

illustrated in Diagram 6-18, which shows what happens when the ball is passed forward out of the trap on the right side. X1, the left guard, retreats to play the left guard position in the 2-1-2 zone. X2, the right guard, drops back to play the right guard position in the zone. X3, the middle man, takes the inside position in the zone. X4, the left forward, plays the left forward position, and X5, the right forward, recovers to assume the right forward position.

THE 2-2-1 THREE-QUARTER "BOXER" ZONE PRESS

Another press we use at three-quarter court is called our "boxer" press. This is a 2-2-1 alignment (Diagram 6-19). We use this as a change of pace when calling audibles on the floor or against teams that attack our presses with a 2-2-1 or 2-3 set. This affords us the opportun-

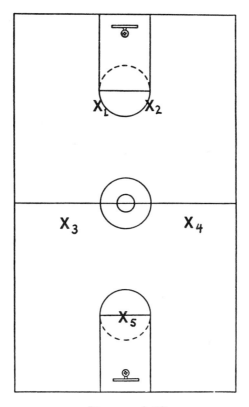

Diagram 6-19

ity to match up with a team and to confuse the opponent when we change our defense from the boxer zone press to a man-to-man press. X1, the left guard, initially lines up at the left side of the key in the back court. He is a trapper when the ball is brought inbounds to his side. X2, the right guard, lines up at the right side of the key in back court and will also be a trapper when the ball is on his side of the floor. X3, the left forward, lines up to the left side of the floor approximately three feet below half court. X4, the right forward, will set up approximately three feet below the half court line on the right side of the floor. X5, the safety man, lines up at the free throw line in the front court.

Diagram 6-20 illustrates the basic defensive coverages we use on the right side against the 2-2-1 offensive set when employing the "boxer" press. X1, the left guard, must turn the dribbler up the sideline into a trap with X3, the left forward, around the area of the

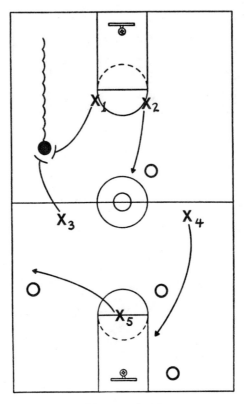

Diagram 6-20

twenty-seven foot hash mark in the back court. X1 has the responsibility of not letting the dribbler break the trap by going between him
and X3. X3 has the responsibility of not letting the dribbler break the
trap by going between him and the sideline. X2, the right guard, will
cover the area around the half court circle and pick off any passes in
this area when the ball is trapped on the right side of the floor. X4, the
right forward, is usually the key man in the "boxer" press when the
ball is on the right side because he most frequently has the responsibility of covering two men in his area. He is an interceptor and must
play "twixt and between" the two men in his area. He is responsible
for this area in the front court around the key. X5, our center, is the
safety man and must stop all passes to the sideline area.

Diagram 6-21 shows the basic defensive slides and coverages
used when the ball is brought up the left side after the inbounds pass
or when an opponent makes a lateral or back pass from the right to the

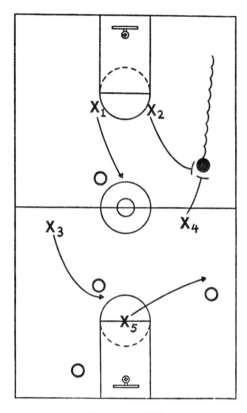

Diagram 6-21

left side. X2, the right guard, forces the ball handler up the left sideline into a double team trap with X4, the right forward. X1, the left guard, assumes the responsibility of covering opponents in the area of the half court circle. X3, the left forward, drops low to cover the opponents in the area around the key in the front. X5, the safety man, will stop all passes to the sideline area.

In backing our press to the three-quarter court level with the "boxer" press, we can press quicker teams. With this press all coverages and slides for each man will be the same at all times. All our player has to do is see which side the ball is on and cover his particular area on that side of the floor. With the boxer press we do away with our middle area trap as in the full court press with the 2-2-1 alignment. This means that our guards must do a super job in turning the ball to the sideline. This press would be a very good press at all levels because it is so simple and will produce results. I have shown this

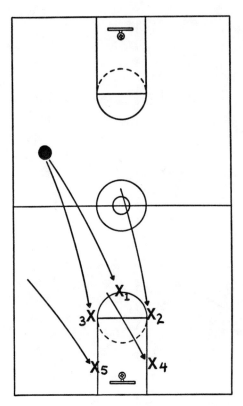

Diagram 6-22

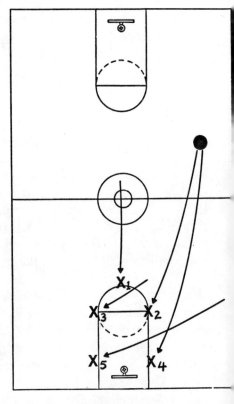

Diagram 6-23

press to elementary and junior high coaches and they have seen tremendous results.

To show another look in our defenses we retreat from the "boxer" press into a 1-2-2 zone defense on all completed forward passes. We feel the 1-2-2 zone provides us an easy method of regrouping. Diagram 6-22 gives an example of our regrouping into the 1-2-2 zone when the ball has been trapped on the right side of the floor. Diagram 6-23 illustrates the regrouping technique we use when the ball has been trapped on the left side of the floor in our "boxer" press.

Chapter 7
Utilizing the
"Slide and Jump"
Half Court Zone
Pressing Defenses

At Cumberland College, we call the half court zone presses our "Slide and Jump" defense. This name is derived from the fundamental methods we use to double team the opponent when he crosses the half court line. Our defensive point man uses the retreat and lateral slide in trapping the opponent and our other trapper literally jumps the opponent the moment he crosses half court.

The types of "slide and jump" half court zone presses that we use are the 2-1-2, 1-2-2, and the 1-3-1. These presses are used throughout the year and have proven to be very beneficial to us.

Like our full court zone presses, our "Slide and Jump" presses are identified by numbers. These numbers describe the type of press we will use when we are calling out audibles on the floor. The following is the number system we use for our half court zone press:

1. 21-5—2-1-2 half court zone press
2. 12-5—1-2-2 half court zone press
3. 13-5—1-3-1 half court zone press

As you can see, the first two digits tell us what alignment we are going to use and the last digit, 5, tells us that it is a half court zone press.

I love the half court zone press because matching up with an opponent's offense is simple. By scouting an opponent or by watching an opponent set its offense up, we know whether they are using a 2-1-2, 1-2-2, or 1-3-1 offensive set. When we see this, we can easily match our zone press alignment with their offensive alignment.

ADVANTAGES OF THE HALF COURT ZONE PRESS

The primary advantage of our half court zone press has been that it has kept opponents from holding the ball on us in the waning moments of the ball game. Several times my teams have been behind two or three points in the final two minutes of the game with the opponent holding the ball. I recall one instance when we were behind by two points with less than a minute to play. We called for our 2-1-2 "slide and jump" press. By continually attacking their stall offense with this press they coughed up two turnovers and a foul in this final minute and we finally won by four points. I must also note that during this time the opponent never took a shot. We demolished the stall.

The "slide and jump" zone presses take advantage of teams fundamentally poor in their passing and ball handling ability. They force these teams to handle the ball under pressure and to throw the ball out of double team situations thus causing numerous mistakes.

Continually changing up the "slide and jump" presses harasses and upsets the opposing teams. Nothing is more disconcerting to an opponent than seeing his pass stolen and laid into the basket. It is also disconcerting at times when a team does not know what press to look for.

The slide and jump zone presses provide the opportunity for more players to play. It is very hard for a player in high school to play a pressing game for thirty-two minutes without a rest. It is even harder on a college player to play a pressing game the whole game because this calls for his playing for forty minutes. Therefore, coaches must utilize their benches. I have found that the more people a coach can play the better his team will be because of that big word —SPIRIT. The more people that feel part of a ball club the more team spirit and dedication for winning a coach will receive.

THE 2-1-2 "SLIDE AND JUMP" HALF COURT ZONE PRESS

21-5 is our 2-1-2 "slide and jump" half court zone press. In one season this press was responsible for 218 turnovers by itself. Naturally, I fell in love with it. In one game that year we started out with this press and through its use we were leading twelve to zero right off the bat.

The initial alignment for our 2-1-2 "slide and jump" half court zone press is illustrated in Diagram 7-1.

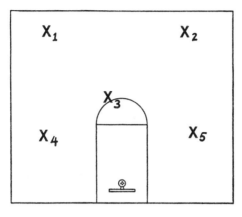

Diagram 7-1

The following are the individual characteristics and position responsibilities of each defensive player in the press. X1 and X2 are guards. They will be trappers when the ball is on their side of the floor. Their initial alignment is two to three steps back of the half court line.

X4 and X5 are forwards. X4 initially lines up on the left side of the floor approximately half way between the free throw line if it were extended and the left sideline. X5 lines up on the right side of the floor approximately half way between the free throw line if it were extended and the right sideline. They are primarily interceptors and must cut off the passing lanes in their areas.

X3 is the center. He initially lines up at the top of the key and usually has the responsibility of fronting the opponents' post man.

Primarily we use our 21-5 press against teams that use a 2-1-2 offensive set (Diagram 7-2). The defensive slides and coverages used in the 2-1-2 "slide and jump" zone press against the 2-1-2 offensive set are shown in Diagram 7-3.

In our 21-5 press we use a different trapping technique than used in the previous presses described. Instead of forcing the ball to the sideline we want the dribbler forced somewhat to the middle. X1, the left defensive guard, forces the dribbler coming up his side of the

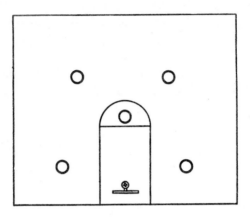

Diagram 7-2

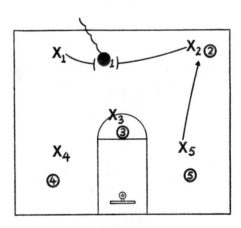

Diagram 7-3

floor to the middle while the offside defensive guard, X2, sags to the middle jumping the dribbler for a double-team with X1. X4, the onside defensive forward, seals off the passing lane in his sideline area. The key to the success of this press when the ball is trapped on the left side usually relies upon X5, the offside defensive forward. It is a must that he pick up the opponents' offside guard, 02, because this man will immediately go to 01's aid and be the most vulnerable receiver. He must always anticipate the double team by X1 and X2 to get a jump on picking up the receiver, 02. It is also necessary that X1 and X2 trap the dribbler sufficiently. This can only come about through daily practice and hard work. X3, the defensive post man, must front anyone in the high post area.

The only pass that the offensive receiver should be able to make is a difficult one. This is a cross court pass from 01 to 05. (Diagram 7-4.) We feel that all cross court passes should be ours because of the length of time that the ball is in the air. If the trappers, X1 and X2, execute their trap properly, it will force 01 to make a lob pass which is what we want. X3 is close enough to intercept this lob pass if it occurs. He must watch the man in the trap and when he sees that the ball is going to 05, he anticipates the pass and intercepts it when it is thrown. Very few times have we not been able to pick this pass off.

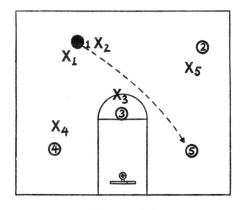

Diagram 7-4

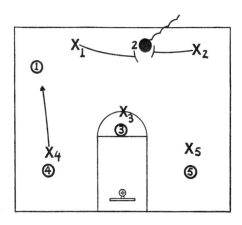

Diagram 7-5

Diagram 7-5 illustrates the slides and defensive coverages of our 21-5 "slide and jump" zone presses to the right side. X2, the right defensive guard, forces the dribbler to the inside; and X1, the left defensive guard, jumps him as he crosses the half court line initiating the double team. X5, the right defensive forward, seals off the pass to the sideline. X3, the defensive post man, overplays his man at the high post area. X4, the left defensive forward, anticipates the pass to the offensive guard and must cut off this passing lane.

The regrouping rule is the same as in our other passes. Unless we are behind or need the ball desperately, we will back up into a standard defense on the first forward pass. From the 21-5 "slide and jump" press we usually regroup into a 2-1-2 zone as shown in Diagram 7-6.

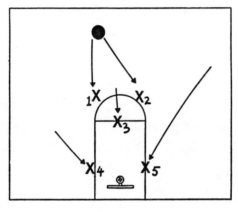

Diagram 7-6

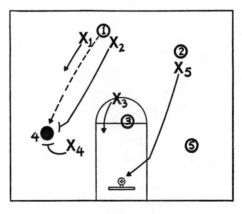

Diagram 7-7

If we are behind or desperately want the basketball, we use a sideline trap. Diagram 7-7 illustrates the sideline trap we use in our 21-5 "slide and jump" press when the ball is on the left side of the floor. X4, the left defensive forward, upon seeing the pass completed to the man in his area, 04, jumps to his outside shoulder forcing him toward the middle for a double team with X2, the right defensive guard. X1, the left defensive guard, must now seal the pass-off back to the offensive guard, 01. He must also anticipate any pass to 02, who is farthest removed from the ball, and go for the interception if the pass is attempted to him. X3, the defensive post man, must play between his man, 03, and the basketball. X5, the right defensive forward, must help seal off the lane area inside. We feel that once the ball has penetrated this far we must cut off passes to the scoring area or the opponents are likely to make easy shots.

The sideline trap on the right side is shown in Diagram 7-8. X1, the left defensive guard, and X5, the right defensive forward, trap the ball on the right side. X3, the defensive post man, cuts off the pass to the high post area. X2, the right defensive guard, seals off passes back to the perimeter area. X4, the left defensive forward, helps cut off passes to the scoring area.

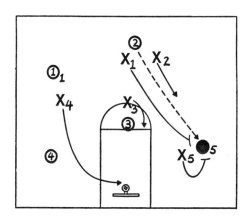

Diagram 7-8

In our "slide and jump" presses we utilize a trap that is not used in our full court and three-quarter court presses. This is a baseline trap. It has been very beneficial to us when we are behind or in dire need of the ball.

Diagram 7-9 illustrates the slides and coverages of the baseline trap from our 21-5 slide and jump zone press when the ball is on the left side. The baseline trap actually goes into effect when X4, the left defensive forward, cannot force 04 to the middle for a sideline

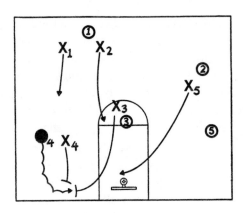

Diagram 7-9

trap with the defensive guard, X1. When instead of going to the inside 04 goes to the baseline, the baseline trap is on. X4 follows the dribbler to the baseline and converges for the double team with X3, who jumps the dribbler after leaving the high post area. X2, the right defensive guard, must cover the high post area when the baseline trap is in effect. X1, the left defensive guard, must stop passes back out to the outside. X5, the right defensive forward, helps seal off the low post area not allowing penetration here. Diagram 7-10 shows that

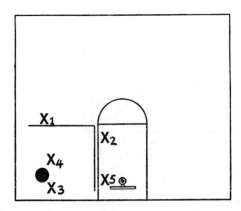

Diagram 7-10

when executing the baseline trap properly, the defense has formed a cup around all vulnerable passing areas hoping for an interception.

Diagram 7-11 illustrates the defensive coverages for the baseline trap on the right side in our 21-5 "slide and jump" press. X5, the right

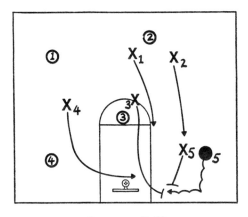

Diagram 7-11

defensive forward, and X3, the defensive post man, trap the dribbler, 05, at the baseline. X4, the left defensive forward, seals off the low post area in the scoring lane. X2, the right defensive guard, stops the pass back outside. X1, the left defensive guard, stops the pass into the high post area.

THE 1-2-2 "SLIDE AND JUMP" HALF COURT ZONE PRESS

We use the 1-2-2 "slide and jump" zone press or our 12-5 press against teams that attack us with some type of 1-2-2 offensive set. We also use this press when our scouting reports show a weakness in a team attacking the 1-2-2 half court zone press.

Diagram 7-12 illustrates the initial alignment of the 1-2-2 "slide and jump" half court zone press. We use this press after a successful field goal or free throw, or by the use of audibles after an unsuccessful goal.

X1, the defensive point man, lines up within the half court circle. He will be a trapper. X2, the left defensive wing man, sets up four to five steps from the sideline on the left side of the floor near the hash mark. He will be a trapper when the ball crosses half court on his side of the floor. X3, the right defensive wing man, initially lines up four to five steps from the sideline on the right side of the floor near the hash mark. He will trap the ball when it crosses half court on the right side of the floor. X4, the left defensive safety man, lines up on the left side of the floor approximately half way between the sideline and the

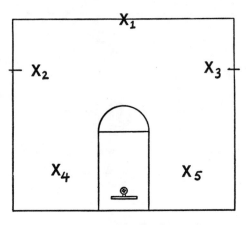

Diagram 7-12

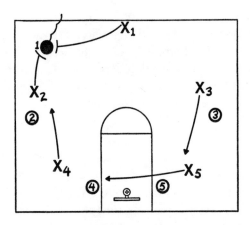

Diagram 7-13

outside of the free throw lane. He will primarily be an interceptor. X5, the right defensive safety man, lines up in this same area but on the right side of the floor and will also be an interceptor.

Diagram 7-13 illustrates the defensive slides and coverages we use when we trap the ball on the left side of the floor in the 12-5 "slide and jump" press as soon as the dribbler crosses the half court line. X1, the defensive point man, forces the dribbler away from the middle toward the sideline. X2, the left defensive wing man, converges with X1 for the double team. X4, the left defensive safety man, has sideline responsibility and must cut off the pass to 02. X5, the right defensive safety man, must protect the basket on the side of the ball so he seals off the passing lane to 04 in the low post area. X3, the right defensive wing man, now has two men to cover. Since they are both farther away from the ball than the other offenders, he can play "twixt and between" them until he anticipates and picks out the one he thinks will be the most vulnerable receiver. He does this by watching the passers' eyes and by watching 03 and 05 cut to the ball. When he sees where the ball is going to be thrown, he goes for the interception.

Diagram 7-14 illustrates the defensive slides and coverages of our 1-2-2 "slide and jump" half court zone press when the dribbler brings the ball up the right side of the floor and is trapped after crossing the half court line. X1, the defensive point man, and X3, the right defensive wing man, trap the ball handler when he crosses half court. X2, the left defensive wing man, has two men in his area and plays in between them anticipating the pass to either of them. X4, the left safety man, protects the basket on the ball side of the floor. X5, the right defensive safety man, has sideline responsibility to stop the pass to the offender, 03.

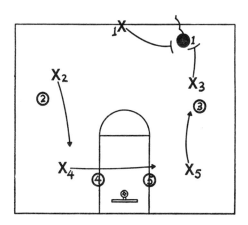

Diagram 7-14

The regrouping technique we use primarily with our 1-2-2 half court zone press is the standard 1-2-2 zone. An example of this regrouping technique is illustrated in Diagram 7-15.

The sideline trap that we use only when we are behind or desperately wanting the basketball is shown in Diagram 7-16 with the ball on the left side of the floor. This trap usually occurs after the ball has been passed from the guard, 01, to the wing, 02. X4, the left defensive safety man, immediately gets between his man, 02, who receives the pass, and the baseline, forcing the opponent to the mid-

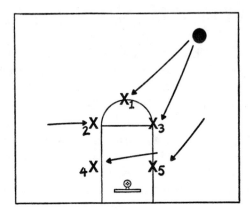

Diagram 7-15

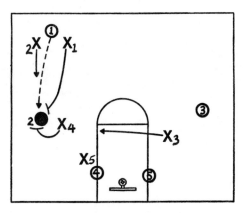

Diagram 7-16

dle. As he does this, X1, the defensive point man, converges with him for the double team. X2, the left defensive wing man, seals off the pass back out to the offensive guard, 01. X5, the right defensive safety man, protects the basket on the ball side of the floor. X3, the right defensive wing man, helps seal off the scoring area by protecting the high post area and picking up any opponent that comes into this area.

Diagram 7-17 shows the shifts for the right sideline trap from our 1-2-2 "slide and jump" half court zone press. X1, the defensive point man and X5, the right defensive safety man, double team the ball. X3, the right defensive forward, stops the pass back to the guard. X2, the left defensive forward, seals off the high post area. X4, the left defensive safety man, denies passes to the low post area.

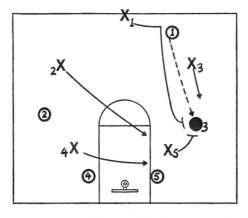

Diagram 7-17

THE 1-3-1 "SLIDE AND JUMP" HALF COURT ZONE PRESS

A half court zone press that is similar to the 1-2-2 is the 1-3-1 half court zone press. We also call this press our 13-5 "slide and jump" press.

We trap the ball at three different areas in this press. First, we trap the ball as soon as it crosses the half court line. We also use the sideline and baseline traps when we desperately want the basketball.

Diagram 7-18 illustrates the initial alignment for our 1-3-1 "slide and jump" half court zone press. We use this press after a successful field goal or free throw against teams that attack us in the front court

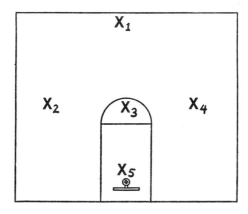

Diagram 7-18

with a 1-3-1 offensive set or against teams that are weak combatting this press. X1, the defensive point man and one of our guards, sets up within the half court circle and traps the ball when the dribbler crosses half court. X2, the left wing, is a forward and sets up about half way between the top of the key in the front court and at the sideline on the left side of the floor. He traps the ball when it crosses half court on his side of the floor and is an interceptor when the ball crosses half court away from him.

X4, the right wing, is also a forward. He initially lines up about half way between the top of the key in the front court and at the sideline on the right side of the floor. He is also a trapper when the ball is brought up his side of the floor and an interceptor when it is away from him.

X3, the defensive post man or middle man, is a guard. He must be quick and able to anticipate passes for interceptions. He lines up around the free throw lane area in the front court.

X5, the safety man, is our center and protects the basket. We want him to reject shots and make penetrators think twice before coming inside.

Diagram 7-19 illustrates the defensive slides and coverages we use in our 1-3-1 "slide and jump" half court zone press when the ball is brought up the left side of the floor. X1, the defensive point man, must force the dribbler, 01, toward the sideline after he crosses the half court line. After the dribbler has come about four steps across half court, X2, the left wing, converges with X1 for the trap. If the dribbler gives up his dribbler before X2 converges, every defender will

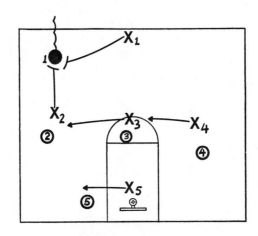

Diagram 7-19

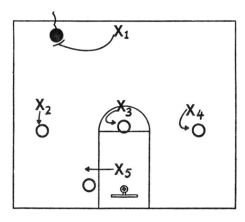

Diagram 7-20

overplay the man in his area (Diagram 7-20). X3, the middle man, has sideline responsibility and assumes this role as soon as he sees X2 leave for the trap. X4, the right wing, sprints to the top of the key and will pick up the most vulnerable receiver in this area, which will be 03 or 04, depending on their movement to the ball. X5, the safety man, protects the basket thus stopping the pass to 05.

Diagram 7-21 illustrates the slides and defensive coverages of the 1-3-1 "slide and jump" half court zone press when the ball is trapped across half court on the right side. X1, the defensive point man, and X4, the right wing, trap the ball approximately four steps past the half court line. X3, the middle man, has sideline responsibility on the right side. X2, the left wing, goes to the top of the key and picks up

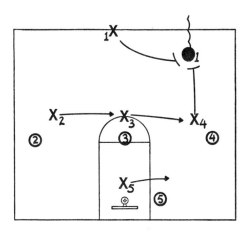

Diagram 7-21

either 02 or 03. His rule is is to pick up the most vulnerable receiver in this area. The key is to watch their offensive movements and the passer's eyes. X5, the safety man, protects the basket.

The sideline trap we use when the ball is on the left side of the floor in our 13-5 "slide and jump" press is illustrated in Diagram 7-22. Again, we use a different trapping technique to fool the opponents, hoping to harass and upset them psychologically. One of the most enjoyable practice days I have ever had was the first day I installed this in one of our practice sessions at Cumberland College. I had my assistant coach take the offensive group downstairs for a skull session. While they were downstairs, I taught this press to a defensive group. This defensive group caused steals time after time because the offensive group was not used to the type of double team technique we had employed.

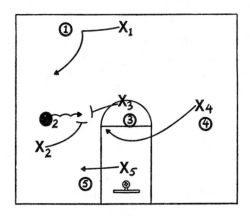

Diagram 7-22

As soon as the offensive wing man, 02, gets the ball, X2, the left defensive wing man, must force the dribbler to the middle of the floor. As soon as he forces the dribbler to the middle, X3, the middle man, converges for the trap. X4, the right wing, sprints to the high post area cutting off this pass. X1, the defensive point man, stops the pass back out to the guard, 01. X5, the safety man, protects the basket, stopping the pass to 05.

Diagram 7-23 shows the sideline trap on the right side of the floor in our 1-3-1 "slide and jump" half court zone press. X4, the right defensive wing, forces the dribbler to the middle into a trap with X3, the middle man, X1, the defensive point man stops the pass back to

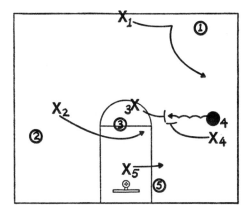

Diagram 7-23

the outside. X2, the left wing seals off the high post area. X5, the safety man, protects the basket area stopping the pass to 05.

If the dribbler takes the baseline instead of going to the middle, the baseline trap immediately goes into effect. Diagram 7-24 illustrates the baseline trap in our 1-3-1 "slide and jump" half court zone press when the ball is on the left side of the floor. X2, the left wing,

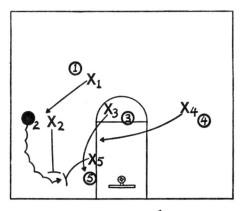

Diagram 7-24

trails the dribbler to the baseline and double teams the ball with X5, the safety man, when he jumps the dribbler at the baseline. X3, the middle man, slides to the low post area protecting the basket as the dribbler, 02, drives the baseline. X4, the right wing, slides into the lane area near the medium post to the ball side of the floor sealing off the pass in this area. X1, the defensive point man, stops the pass back outside to 01.

The baseline trap from the 13-5 "slide and jump" press is shown in Diagram 7-25 with the ball on the right side of the floor. X4, the right defensive wing, trails the dribbler to the baseline and traps the ball with X5, the safety man. X3, the middle man, slides to the low post area protecting the basket and fronting 05. X2, the left defensive wing, slides across to the medium post area on the ball side of the floor stopping any pass into this area. X1, the defensive point man, does not let the pass come back outside to 01, the offensive guard.

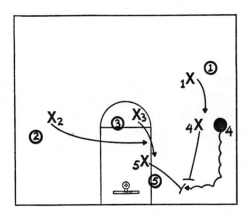

Diagram 7-25

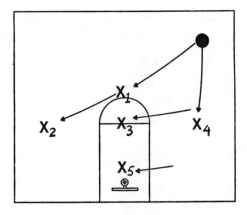

Diagram 7-26

The regrouping technique we primarily use in our 1-3-1 half court zone press is the standard 1-3-1 zone defense. An example of regrouping from a trap on the right side of the floor is shown in Diagram 7-26. As you can see, this is a simple regrouping technique.

Chapter 8
Regrouping after the Zone Press with the Standard Zone Defenses

The zone defenses have played a major role in our defensive strategies in the past years. It is my philosophy to use as many defenses as possible. Every defense used against an opponent means another he must be prepared for. If he is not prepared for a certain defense, he is likely to be beaten. We use the standard zone defenses to allow us to use more defensive strategies and regroup after a zone press.

We have found that it is much easier to back up into a zone defense after a press than to back up into a man-to-man defense. This is because it is much easier for a player to go to a certain area of the floor he is responsible for than it is to hunt and find a specific opponent. This loss of time in finding an opponent can allow the opponent to beat a press. Backing up to this zone defense area is quicker; thus the press will not be broken as often.

The zone defenses we use are the 1-3-1, 2-1-2, and the 1-2-2. We have used these defenses many times as a primary defense. We have played many teams who were weak shooting from the outside or who have trouble combatting one of these defenses. When we play these types of teams, we employ the standard zone defense they are weakest against as our primary half court defense.

At Cumberland College one season we had to play a conference opponent who was extremely quick against the man-to-man defense. We scouted them the week before we played them and found a weakness in their attacking of the 2-1-2 zone defense. By using the 2-1-2 zone as our primary defense we won the game by six points.

THE 2-1-2 ZONE DEFENSE

This defense has been a favorite of many coaches for a long time. We use this defense primarily for regrouping after the 2-1-2 zone press either at the full court or three-quarter court level. We have used this defense against teams that are weak shooting from the wing area. We have also received beneficial results from the 2-1-2 zone when we are changing up defense through the use of audibles.

The initial alignment of the 2-1-2 zone defense we use for regrouping purposes is shown in Diagram 8-1. From the zone press each player has been assigned a specific area to regroup into if the offense has penetrated the press. X1 and X2 are always our guards; X4 and X5 are our forwards; and X3 is our center.

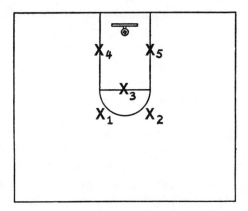

Diagram 8-1

We usually back into this defense when the offensive team completes the first forward pass against the press. Our players believe that even if a team breaks the press they still must break our zone defense to score.

When the ball is at the wing area, we shift our players in the 2-1-2 zone in two basic ways. One shift is called the guard coverage and the other our forward coverage. The zone shifts we use when utilizing our guard coverage are illustrated in Diagram 8-2 with the ball at the wing area on the right side.

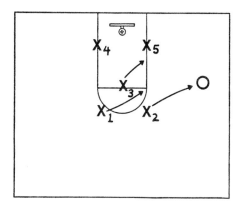

Diagram 8-2

X2, the right guard, applies pressure on the ball and, if the opponent shoots, yells "shot," notifying all players to block out and get the defensive rebound. X1, the left guard, slides to the side of the ball sealing off the passing lane to the high post area. X3, the defensive post man, overplays opponents in the medium post area not letting a pass come in here. X5, the right forward, cuts off the passing lane at the low post area on the ball side of the floor. X4, the left forward, is responsible for the offside rebound if the shot is taken and tries to intercept any cross court passes made.

If a shot is taken from this wing area, we want a cup formed around the goal for defensive rebounding (Diagram 8-3). If the cup is formed properly and the fundamentals of blocking out are executed, we should have ninety-five per cent of all missed shots.

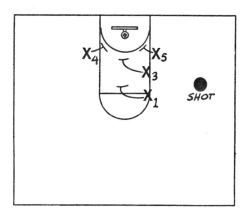

Diagram 8-3

X2, the right guard, should block the shooter out. X1, the left guard, is responsible for the long rebound near the free throw line. The cup is formed around the goal by X3, the defensive post man, X4, the left forward, and X5, the right forward. X3 is responsible for all short rebounds in front of the goal. X4 should have rebounds that come off the left side of the goal. X5 should have all rebounds that come off on the right side.

The guard coverage technique we use when the ball is at the wing area on the left side is shown in Diagram 8-4.

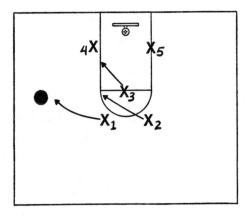

Diagram 8-4

X1, the left guard, applies pressure on the ball. X2, the right guard, stops passes to the high post area. X3, the defensive post man, seals off the passing lane to the medium post area. X4, the left forward, keeps the pass from penetrating into the low post area. X5, the right forward, picks off all cross court passes and is responsible for the offside rebound.

The weakness in our defense with the guard coverage is allowing the shot at the wing area. If a team makes our two defensive guards commit themselves (Diagram 8-5) into picking the offensive guard out front, the shot from the wing area is easy to take after a pass from out front. This is okay against a team that is weak shooting at this area, but what about a team that starts hitting their shots from this area? Within this question lies the reason we installed our forward coverage of the wing area in the 2-1-2 zone (Diagram 8-6). We found that we must stop the team that gets a hot shooting hand in the wing area. The forward coverage is the quickest method of covering the wing area

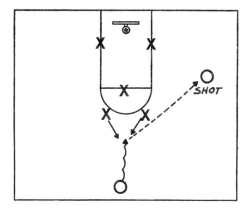

Diagram 8-5

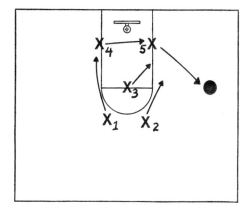

Diagram 8-6

because the forward can anticipate the pass to this area and sprint to the wing. In the guard coverage, the guards have to use a lateral or retreat slide to get to the wing, and this is much slower than the sprint.

In the forward coverage, X5, the right forward, defenses the opponent with the ball. X2, the right guard, seals off the passing to the high post area and is responsible for long rebounds near the free throw line when the shot is taken. X3, the defensive post man, stops passes to the medium post area and should get all rebounds that come off the front of the basket. X4, the left forward, fills the low post area to the side of the ball and should get the rebounds that come off on the right side. X2, X3 and X5 should use the defensive technique of playing between the man in their areas and the basketball. X1, the left guard, slides down low getting the offside rebound if a shot is taken.

Diagram 8-7 illustrates our forward coverage of the left wing area in the 2-1-2 zone. X4, the left forward, applies pressure on the ball. X1, the left guard, seals off the high post area and gets long rebounds near the free throw line. X3, the defensive post man, stops passes into the medium post area. X5, the right forward, overplays opponents in the low post area. X2, the right guard, slides low away from the ball and picks up cross court passes and offside rebounds. The defensive rebounding cup is formed by X5, X3 and X2 with X5 taking the left side, X3 the middle, and X2 the right side.

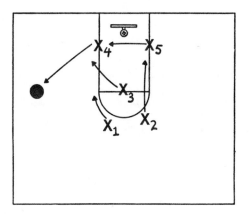

Diagram 8-7

The defensive shifts in our 2-1-2 zone defense that we always use when the ball is in the right corner are illustrated in Diagram 8-8.

Passes to the high post area are cut off by X2, the right guard. Passes to the medium post area are cut off by X3, the defensive post man. Passes to the low post area are stopped by X4, the left forward. As you can see, we definitely believe that the ball should never come inside. X5, the right forward, applies pressure to the ball. X1, the left guard, has offside rebounding responsibility and stops all cross court passes that are attempted. The defensive rebounding cup inside is formed by X1, X3, and X4. X1 has the left side, X3 the middle, and X4 the right side.

Corner coverage on the left side of the floor in our 2-1-2 zone is illustrated in Diagram 8-9. X1, the left guard, does not let the ball come into the high post area and is responsible for the long rebound

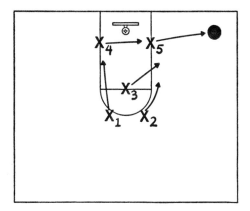

Diagram 8-8

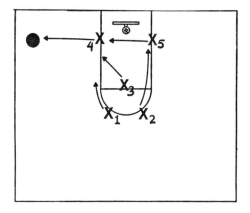

Diagram 8-9

near the free throw line. X4, the left forward, applies pressure on the ball. X5, the right forward, stops passes to the low post area and is responsible for left side rebounds in our defensive rebounding cup. X3, the defensive post man, fronts the medium post area, and is responsible for the middle area in our rebounding cup. X2, the right guard, stops all cross court passes and is responsible for offside rebounding on the right side of the defensive cup.

THE 1-2-2 ZONE DEFENSE

Many times we have used the 1-2-2 zone defense for regrouping after opponents break a zone press. We also use the 1-2-2 zone defense against teams that are strong shooting from the outside but are weak in the middle.

The 1-2-2 initial alignment we set up in after a press is illustrated in Diagram 8-10. X1, the defensive point man, is our quickest guard and lines up at the top of the key. X2, the left wing, is a guard and lines up at the left side of the free throw line. Most teams start their offense on their right side of the floor. Therefore, we want a good defensive man covering this wing area. X3, the right wing, is a weak side forward and must be a good rebounder. He sets up at the edge of the free throw line on the right side.

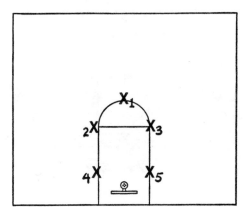

Diagram 8-10

X4, the left baseline man, is our best rebounding forward and initially sets up in the low post area on the left side of the goal. X5, the right baseline man, is the center. Most of the rebounds will come off on his side of the floor so we want our best rebounder in this area. This is because most teams attack us offensively away from his side of the floor. He lines up after the press in the low post area on the right side of the goal.

When we have lined up in the 1-2-2 zone after a team has penetrated our press, the players must play with aggressiveness and fire. We must make the opposing players earn their baskets. If they break the press and then break the zone defense, they have done a beautiful job of executing their plans because we are not going to give them anything.

The defensive shifts we use in the 1-2-2 zone defense when the ball is out front on the left side of the defense are shown in Diagram

8-11. When the ball is here, X2, the left wing and X4, the left baseline man, keep any man from getting the ball in their areas. X1, the defensive point man, takes the man with the ball and tries to make him give up his dribble without making our left wing, X2, commit himself defensively to the dribbler. This allows X2 to stop penetration into the high post area from outside. X3, the right wing, slides to the middle of the free throw line picking up the nearest receiver in this area and keeping him from getting the ball. X5, the right baseline man, slides up into the lane two to three steps toward the ball looking for a vulnerable receiver.

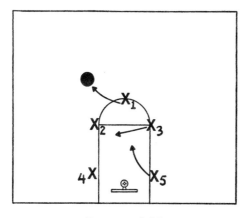

Diagram 8-11

Diagram 8-12 shows the defensive shifts from the 1-2-2 zone when the ball is out front on the other side of the floor. X3, the right wing, and X5, the right baseline man, hold in their area stopping the pass inside. X2, the left wing, shifts to the middle of the free throw line stopping passes to the high post. X1, the defensive point man, applies pressure on the ball. X4, the left baseline man, slides up into the lane two to three steps, picking up the nearest receiver.

The defensive rebounding cup we form when the ball is shot from out front to the left side is shown in Diagram 8-13, and the right side rebounding cup is in Diagram 8-14. The defensive shifts in the 1-2-2 zone when the ball is at the left side of our defense at the wing area are illustrated in Diagram 8-15. X1, the left wing, seals off the passing lane to the high post area. X2, the left wing, defenses the opponent with the basketball. X4, the left baseline man, stays in his initial alignment area covering any man coming into this low post

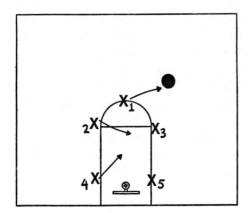

Diagram 8-12

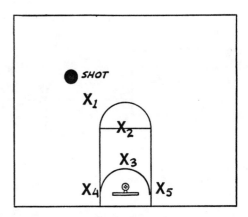

Diagram 8-13

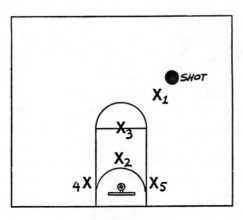

Diagram 8-14

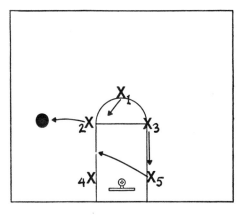

Diagram 8-15

area. X5, the right baseline man, shifts up to the medium post area stopping the ball coming to an opponent in this area. X3, the right wing, slides down the lane to assume the offside rebounding responsibility and intercept cross court passes.

Diagram 8-16 shows the rebounding cup we use when the ball is shot from the wing area.

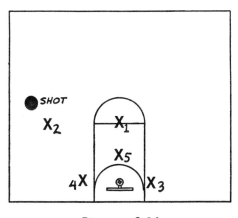

Diagram 8-16

When the ball is at the other wing area against the 1-2-2 zone we shift to the positions shown in Diagram 8-17. X3, the right wing, plays the man with the ball tight. X1, the defensive point man, covers the high post area. X4, the left baseline man, stops penetration of the pass to the medium post area. X5, the right baseline man, defenses any

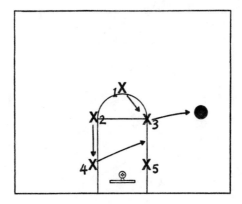

Diagram 8-17

man in the low post area. X2, the left wing, assumes offside rebounding responsibility and tries to pick off cross court passes.

The defensive rebounding cup formed from shots in this area is pictured in Diagram 8-18.

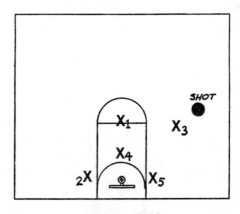

Diagram 8-18

Diagram 8-19 illustrates the defensive shifts of the 1-2-2 zone when the ball is in the corner on the left side of the defense. X4, the left baseline man, defenses the man with the ball. X5, the right baseline man, fills X4's vacated spot, stopping any pass to an opponent in the low post area. X2, the left wing, seals off the passing lane to the medium post area. X1, the defensive point man, keeps the pass from coming into the high post area. X3, the right wing, is responsible for the offside rebound and can pick off cross court passes.

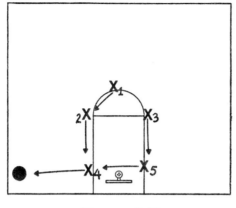

Diagram 8-19

The defensive rebounding cup is pictured in Diagram 8-20.

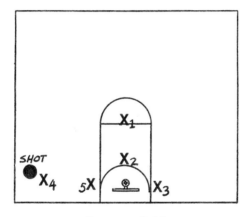

Diagram 8-20

Defensive responsibilities of the players in the 1-2-2 zone when the ball is in the corner on the other side of the floor are illustrated in Diagram 8-21. X5, the right baseline man, defenses the man with the ball. X4, the left baseline man, has the responsibility of defensing an opponent in the low post area. X3, the right wing, stops passes to the medium post area. X1, the defensive point man, seals off the passing lane to the high post area. X2, the left wing, has offside rebounding responsibility and picks off cross court passes.

It must be noted that in all of our zones, the defensive men covering the high post, medium post, and low post areas play between the man in their respective areas and the basketball.

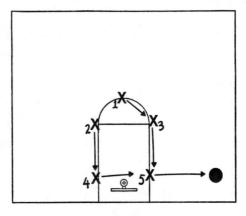

Diagram 8-21

The defensive rebounding cup from the right corner area is shown in Diagram 8-22.

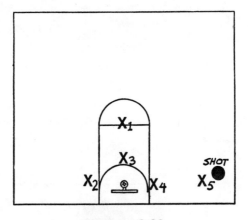

Diagram 8-22

THE 1-3-1 ZONE

Probably the most popular zone defense in the past five years of my coaching career has been the 1-3-1 zone. We use it for regrouping after an opponent breaks our 1-2-1-1 full court zone press, 1-2-1-1 three-quarter court press, or the 1-3-1 half court zone press. We also use this as a primary defense if our scouting reports call for it.

The defensive player alignment for the 1-3-1 zone is shown in Diagram 8-23. X1, the defensive point man, is one of the guards. He

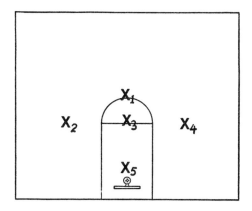

Diagram 8-23

sets up at the top of the key. X2, the left wing, is a forward and lines up about two to three steps to the left side of the free throw line. X3, the defensive post man, is our center. His initial alignment is around the middle of the free throw line. X4, the right wing, is our other forward and lines up two to three steps to the right side of the free throw line. X5, the baseline man, is our quickest guard because he has the responsibility of covering all of the baseline area. He regroups into the 1-3-1 zone directly under the basket.

Diagram 8-24 illustrates player responsibilities and coverages with the ball out front to the left of the defense. In describing our 1-3-1 zone techniques, I am going to use a 2-1-2 offensive set as an example of what can be defensed.

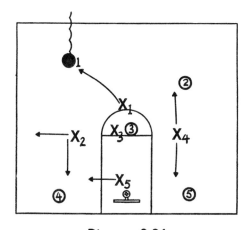

Diagram 8-24

X1, the defensive point man, has the responsibility of stopping the basketball as soon as the dribbler, 01, crosses half court. As soon as X1 makes 01 give up his dribble, X2, the left wing, has the responsibility of stopping the pass to the wing or corner on his side. In this case, he would stop any pass from 01 to 04. X3, the defensive post man, must front the opponent, 03, in the high post area. X5, the baseline man, moves to the edge of the foul lane near the baseline on the side of the ball. He is to anticipate any long pass from 01 to his receivers. In this case he would watch for the pass from 01 to 04 or from 01 to 05. X4, the right wing, is our gambler. He is away from the ball and has two men, 02 and 05, on his side of the floor. He watches the passer's, 01's, eyes to see which receiver 01 is going to pass to. He gambles on this anticipation and awaits the pass to the most vulnerable receiver.

The defensive coverages and player responsibilities when the ball is out front on the right side of our defense are illustrated in Diagram 8-25.

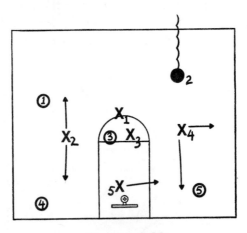

Diagram 8-25

X1, the defensive point man, makes the opponent give up his dribble after crossing the half court line. X4, the right wing, stops the pass to the wing or corner (02 to 05). X3, the defensive post man, plays between his man, 03, and the ball at the high post area. X5, the baseline man, slides to the edge of the foul lane near the baseline on the ball side of the floor trying to pick off long passes made by 01. X2, the left wing, has two men on his side and plays in between them until he discovers the most vulnerable of the receivers, 01 or 04.

If we do not steal the ball from the pass attempted out front and if the ball penetrates to the wing area on the left side of the floor, we use the defensive coverages illustrated in Diagram 8-26. X2, the left wing, defends the opponent with the basketball. X1, the defensive point man, covers any man in the high post area. X3, the defensive post man, is responsible for taking any opponent in the medium post area. X5, the baseline man, stops the pass to the low post area. X4, the right wing has offside rebounding responsibility and intercepts cross court passes.

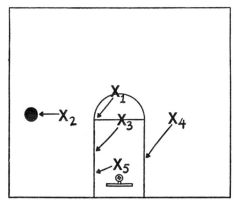

Diagram 8-26

The rebounding cup that is formed when the ball is shot from this area is pictured in Diagram 8-27.

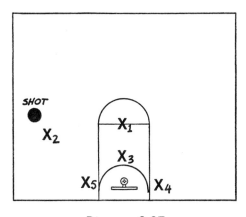

Diagram 8-27

Diagram 8-28 illustrates the right wing area coverage and defensive responsibilities in the 1-3-1 zone.

X4, the right wing, applies pressure on the ball. X1, the defensive point man, seals off the passing lane to the high post area. X3, the defensive post man, stops penetration of the pass into the medium post area. X5, the baseline man, covers the low post area. X2, the left wing, has offside rebounding responsibility and steals cross court passes made by the opponent.

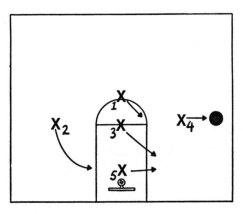

Diagram 8-28

The defensive rebounding cup we form when the ball is shot from this area is pictured in Diagram 8-29.

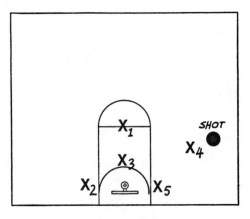

Diagram 8-29

The corner coverage in the 1-3-1 zone is illustrated in Diagram 8-30 with the ball on the left side of the defense. X5, the baseline man, defenses the opponent with the basketball. X3, the defensive post man, stops the pass into the low post area. X2, the left wing, sags back to front any opponent in the medium post area. X1, the defensive point man, stops the pass into the high post area. X4, the right wing, is responsible for getting the offside rebound and intercepting cross court passes.

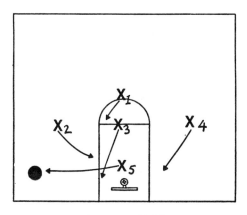

Diagram 8-30

The defensive rebounding cup formed from a shot in this area is pictured in Diagram 8-31.

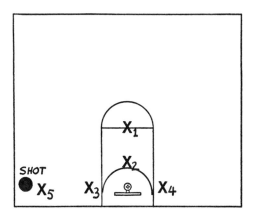

Diagram 8-31

The right corner coverage of the 1-3-1 zone is illustrated in Diagram 8-32. X5, the baseline man, applies pressure on the ball. X3, the defensive post man, covers the low post area. X4, the right wing, sags into the medium post area fronting any opponent here. X1, the defensive point man, seals off the high post area. X2, the left wing, picks off cross court passes and drops low away from the ball for the offside rebound.

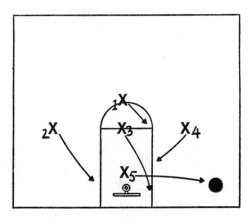

Diagram 8-32

The defensive rebounding cup formed from shots in the right corner is pictured in Diagram 8-33.

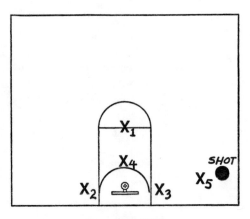

Diagram 8-33

ZONE PRESS TECHNIQUES WITH THE STANDARD ZONE DEFENSES

When I first began coaching the zone press, I saw at times a laxity in our zone defense after we had regrouped. Therefore, I felt if we used some zone press techniques in our zone defenses when this laxity occurred, our defense might be tougher. These techniques proved to be very beneficial to us. We also found that these zone press techniques were effective against control or semi-control teams. At times we have used these techniques against teams that stalled on us in the waning moments of a quarter or half.

Our zone pressing techniques in the 2-1-2 zone are illustrated against a 1-3-1 offensive set since this is the type of offense most teams use to attack this defense. When in the 2-1-2 zone defense, we use zone pressing techniques when the ball is out front and in the corner.

Diagram 8-34 illustrates the zone pressing techniques we use in the 2-1-2 zone with the ball out front. X1 and X2, the defensive guards, make the opponent, 01, pick up his dribble out front. X3, the defensive post man, overplays 03 in the high post area. X4, the left forward, immediately sprints to the left wing area and fronts 02. X5, the right forward, sprints to 04 at the right area and overplays him. It is essential that X1 and X2 do a superb job of double teaming and not let 01 make the good pass to any of the receivers, especially to 05. If he does attempt a high lob pass or makes a bad pass to 05, we can regroup back to our defensive areas without difficulty. Usually when

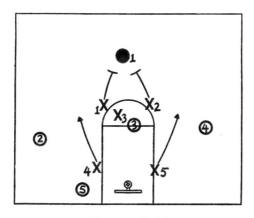

Diagram 8-34

X1 and X2 do the proper job trapping, we will get the basketball if the other defenders assume their responsibilities.

We also trap the ball in the 2-1-2 zone in the corners. This is illustrated in Diagram 8-35 with the ball on the left side of the defense. As soon as the ball goes to this corner, X4, the left forward, has the responsibility of defending the man with the basketball. We tell X4 to give the dribbler the baseline. When the dribbler takes it, X4 trails him until he converges for the double team with X3, the defensive post man. We tell X3 to make his move to double team as soon as the opponent starts the dribble. X3 and X4 have now formed a trap that is very difficult to get out of because all of the passing lanes have been cut off by X5, X2 and X1. X1, the left guard, cuts off the passing lane back to the wing. X2, the right guard, slides to the ball side of the floor sealing off the passing lane to the medium post. X5, the right forward, seals off the low post area.

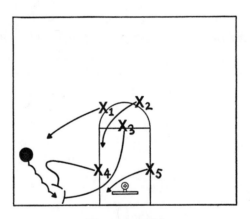

Diagram 8-35

This same technique on the opposite side of the floor is shown in Diagram 8-36. X5, the right forward, and X3, the defensive post man, double team the ball at the baseline. X2, the right guard, stops the pass back to wing area. X4, the left forward, overplays any man in the low post area. X1, the left guard, stops the pass near the medium post area.

At times when in our 1-2-2 zone defense, teams have gotten the ball into the area around the free thow line. Therefore, we felt that this was a good place to put in a zone press technique. The zone press technique we use with the 1-2-2 zone when the ball is passed to an

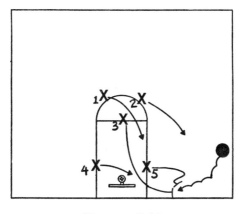

Diagram 8-36

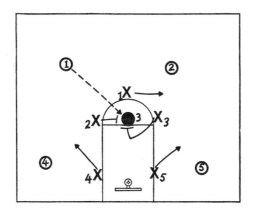

Diagram 8-37

opponent near the free throw line is shown in Diagram 8-37. I will use
a 2-1-2 offensive set as an example because this is a common set
against the 1-2-2 zone. The defensive coverages and player responsibilities are as follows: The wing man to the side of the ball, X2 in this
case, always has the responsibility of helping double team the ball and
of not letting the opponent with the ball pass it back to the side it
came from. Thus, X2 would not let O3 pass the ball back to O1. This
gives X1, the defensive point man, a chance to overshade the most
vulnerable receiver out front, O2. If X2 does not stop the pass from O3
to O1, X1 will have a difficult time stealing the ball. X3, the right
wing, double teams the ball with X2 and establishes a defensive position between the ball, O3, and the basket. X4, the left baseline man,

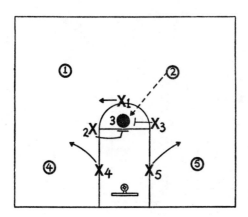

Diagram 8-38

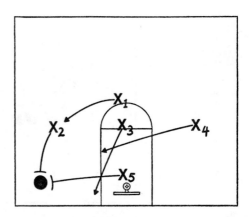

Diagram 8-39

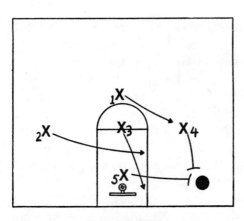

Diagram 8-40

overplays the man, 04, in the wing area on his side. X5, the right baseline man cuts off the pass to 05 at the right wing area.

When the ball is penetrated to the middle from the right side of the defense, the technique we use is described in Diagram 8-38.

X3, the right wing, and X2, the left wing, double team the ball. X2 plays between 03 and the basket. X3 plays to the side of the opponent that the ball came in on and tries to discourage the pass back to 02. X1, the defensive point man, anticipates the pass to 01 and looks for the steal. X4, the left wing, and X5, the right wing, cut off the passes to their wing areas, 04 and 05, respectively.

Diagram 8-39 illustrates a zone pressing technique in the 1-3-1 zone when the ball is in the corner to the left side of our defense. X2, the left wing, and X5, the baseline man, double team the ball in the corner. X1, the defensive point man, does not allow the ball to get back to the wing. X4, the right wing, overplays the opponent nearest to the medium post area. X3, the defensive post man, slides to the low post area defending the nearest receiver in this area.

This technique with the ball to the right side of our 1-3-1 zone is shown in Diagram 8-40. X4, the right wing, and X5, the baseline man, double team the ball. X3, the defensive post man, overplays any man in the low post area. X2, the left wing, picks up the nearest man in the medium post area. X1, the defensive point man, stops the pass from coming back to the wing.

I have seen these zone press techniques put polish on a zone. They are gambles, but that's part of our philosophy!

Chapter 9
Drills to Perfect the
Zone Press

The success of the various zone presses depends upon the amount of time the pressing techniques are practiced. Defensive pressing techniques for a successful pressing team require quickness, timing, and aggressiveness on the part of each player. To develop good zone presses a team must perfect these techniques through the use of drills in daily practice sessions. These drills are of special importance in the pre-season when a coach is teaching his pressing philosophy. Drills are a must in teaching the zone press.

There are many drills we use to perfect our zone presses. We utilize trapping drills, sliding drills, regrouping drills, one-on-one drills, reaction drills, and blocking out drills. These drills are used before the season and during the season to improve the defensive skills that are necessary to the success of our zone presses.

It must be noted that each member of the team needs to perform in each of these drills because at some time during the season each player will be involved with some type of pressing situation defensively.

TRAPPING DRILLS

Full Court Trapping Drills

The double-team trap is necessary for any successful zone press. Diagram 9-1 illustrates the full court trapping drill we use to perfect

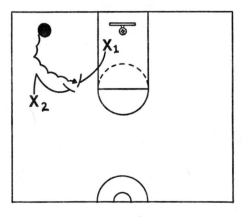

Diagram 9-1

the 1-2-1-1 full court zone presses. As soon as the manager, who is standing at the sideline, blows the whistle, the dribbler heads for the opposite end of the court. X1 and X2, the defensive men, must trap the ball as soon as possible. X2 has the responsibility of forcing the dribbler to the middle towards X1. X2 must not let the dribbler get between him and the sideline. X1 has the responsibility of converging with X2 for the trap and should not let the dribbler break the trap by going between himself and X2. This drill is considered completed and the next group starts the drill when the dribbler breaks the trap or the defensive men double team the ball successfully.

Diagram 9-2 is a full court trapping drill designed to perfect the 2-1-2 full court zone press trapping technique. X1 lines up a couple of

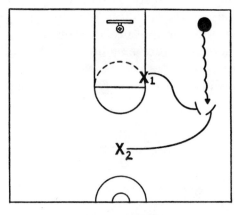

Diagram 9-2

steps below the edge of the free throw line on the right side. X2 sets up approximately half way between the top of the key in the back court and the half court. The offensive player starts at the end line and dribbles toward the opposite end of the floor. X1 forces the dribbler to the sideline not letting the dribbler break through the trap between himself and X2. X2 converges with X1 for the trap and does not let the dribbler go to the outside between himself and the sideline. We want the trap executed in the back court area near the free throw line extended. This drill is also executed on the left side of the floor.

Diagram 9-3 is the drill we use to perfect the 2-2-1 full court zone press trapping technique. X1 lines up at the left edge of the free throw line. X2 lines up six to eight feet above the half court line on the left side of the floor. The offensive man dribbles toward the opposite end of the floor. X1 turns the dribbler to the sideline converging with X2 for the trap near the free throw line extended. X2 keeps the dribbler from going outside of the trap and X1 keeps him from going through the trap.

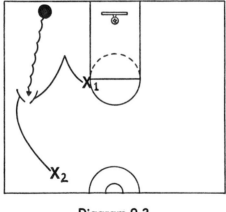

Diagram 9-3

Three-Quarter Court Trapping Drills

Diagram 9-4 illustrates the drill we use to perfect the 1-2-1-1 three-quarter court zone press. The opponent starts his dribble four to five steps from the end line in back court on the left side. X1 lines up in the middle of the free throw line, and X2 lines up two to three steps above the half court line on the left side of the floor. Ideally, the trap will be made near the twenty-seven foot hash mark by X1 and

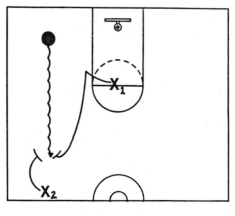

Diagram 9-4

X2. X2 is not to let the dribbler outside the trap, and X1 should not let him go in between the trap. The drill must also be practiced on the other side of the floor.

A drill to perfect the trap in the 2-1-2 three-quarter court zone press is shown in Diagram 9-5. X1 lines up near the top of the key on the right side. X2 lines up at the top of the circle near half court. X1 forces the opponent, who is dribbling to the opposite end of the floor, to the sideline and converges with X2 for the trap. The drill is also practiced on the opposite side of the floor.

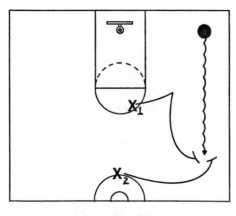

Diagram 9-5

Diagram 9-6 is a trapping drill used to perfect the 2-2-1 three-quarter court zone press. X1 lines up at the left side of the key and

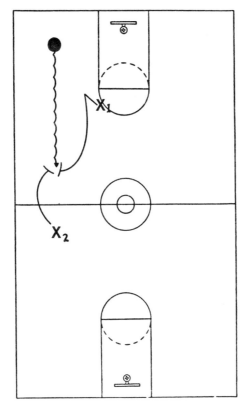

Diagram 9-6

forces the dribbler to the sidelines. X2 sets up two to three steps below half court on the left side and slides up to double team the dribbler with X1. These techniques must also be practiced on the right side.

Half Court Trapping Drills

Diagram 9-7 is a drill we use to improve our defensive trapping techniques in our 1-2-2 and 1-3-1 half court zone presses. We use this drill on both sides of the floor. X1 lines up in the middle of the circle at half court. X2 lines up four to five steps from the sideline on the left side of the floor near the hash mark. The opponent begins his dribble near the hash mark in the back court. X1 and X2 must trap the dribbler immediately after he crosses half court. X1 does not let the dribbler break the trap inside and X2 does not let the opponent break the trap by going to the outside.

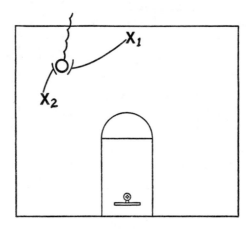

Diagram 9-7

Diagram 9-8 is our 2-1-2 half court trapping drill. X1 and X2 line up two to three steps back of the half court line on their respective sides. The offensive player begins to dribble up court near the hash mark in the back court. X1 is responsible for turning the dribbler towards the middle into a double team with X2 who has converged by laterally sliding from his right side position.

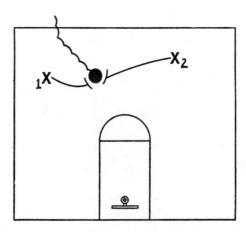

Diagram 9-8

Sideline Trapping Drill

Diagram 9-9 illustrates the drill we use for executing the sideline trap from an initial trap. In this drill 01 passes the ball to 02. X2 will slow 02's penetration toward the goal by playing him head-up and

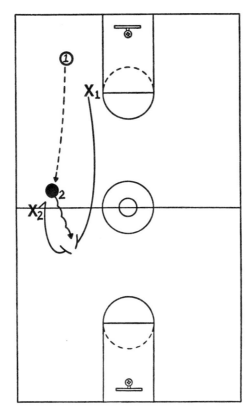

Diagram 9-9

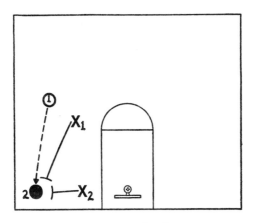

Diagram 9-10

awaits X1 for the double team near the sideline area. X1 releases from 01 as soon as the ball leaves 01's fingertips.

Corner Trapping Drill

The corner trap drill that we use to perfect our zone pressing techniques is shown in Diagram 9-10. 01 passes the ball to 02. X2 applies immediate pressure on the ball while X1 releases from the pass to double team the ball with X2.

SLIDING DRILLS

The Full Court Sliding Drill

The full court sliding drill (Diagram 9-11) is a defensive drill to improve the individual's defensive slides. We want to emphasize good body balance with no unnecessary head and arm movement. The drill starts with the player positioned at a corner of the court area. He gets in a good defensive stance and on the manager or coach's whistle, quickly slides to the end of the free throw line where he will turn to the outside and slide to the corner of the half court area. Now he turns his body to the inside and slides to the other free throw line. Here he will again turn to the outside and slide to the corner of the court opposite where he started. Next he laterally slides across the baseline until he gets to the corner where he turns to the inside and slides to the edge of the free throw line. His next slide is to turn to the outside and slide to the corner of the half court area. He then turns to the inside to slide to the edge of the free throw line. He must then turn his body facing the outside and slide to the corner of the court where he starts his last move—a lateral slide to the area where he began this drill.

The Bulldog Sliding Drill

The Bulldog Sliding Drill (Diagram 9-12) is a defensive sliding drill named after the Cumberland Bulldogs. It is designed for the coaches to watch the individual's feet, head, back, and arm movements while the player slides.

We divide the players into four groups using both ends of the

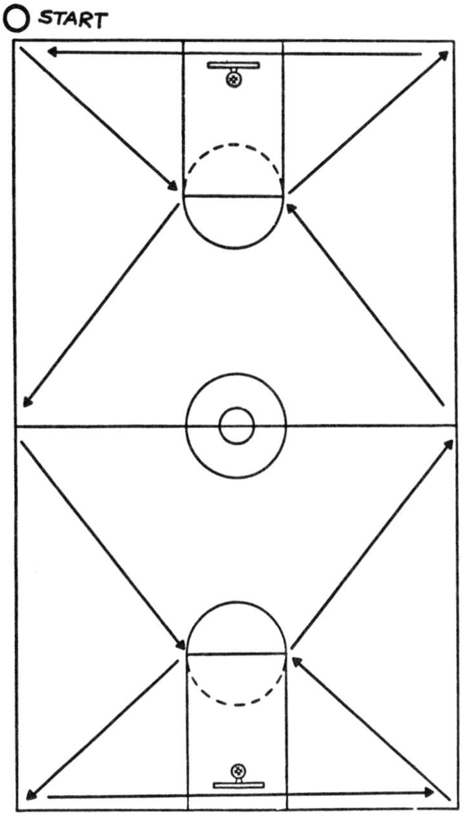

O START

Diagram 9-11

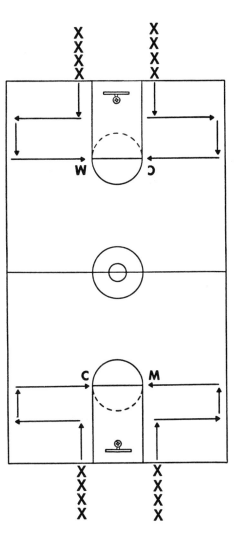

Diagram 9-12

court so that two groups will be at each end. The two groups at each end of the court set up near the basket area about twelve feet apart. Each group will face a coach or manager who will give the player the command to start the drill.

With each group the drill will begin with the individual player getting in a good defensive stance. At the coach or manager's command the player advances toward the coach or manager until he gets half way. The coach signals with the motion of his hand for him to laterally slide to the sideline. From the sideline he uses the forward slide until the coach or manager signals with a hand motion to laterally slide back across the court. After the player completes these slides he will move to the other group on his end of the court and perform his sliding movements in this area.

The Backup Sliding Drill

The backup sliding drill (Diagram 9-13) is designed to improve the players backward movement. This backup slide is a crucial slide because it is one a defender normally uses when an opponent is driving to the basket. The backup sliding drill combines the use of the backward slide and the lateral slide. The individual player positions himself at the half court line facing the coach who is below the half court line. On the coach's whistle the player shuffles backwards. On the second whistle he laterally slides to his left. The third whistle signals the player to slide backwards again until he hears the next whistle which signals the lateral slide to his right. The last slide is a backwards slide to the baseline.

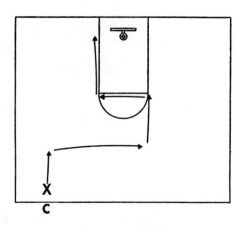

Diagram 9-13

DEFENSIVE REGROUPING DRILLS

"Knight" Full Court Regrouping Drill

The Knight full court regrouping drill (Diagram 9-14) is a drill named after the Ocala Vanguard Knights and is used to teach our backing up principles on defense. We set up in a full court trapping

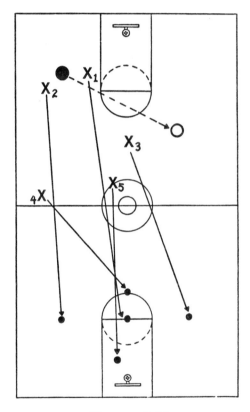

Diagram 9-14

situation defensively. We use two offensive men in the drill. One will be in the trap and will be the passer. The other will be at an area on the floor designated by the coach and will be the receiver. The purpose of this drill is to get the defense to release back to its zone area within three and one-half seconds after the pass leaves the passer's fingertips. We feel our press will not get beat if we are all back within this time limit. The trapping example used in Diagram 9-14 is from the 1-2-1-1 full court zone press. The pass is actually going into X3's area, but he is not allowed to steal ball. The defensive players in this situation are backing up into the 1-3-1 zone which is usually the defense we regroup to after the 1-2-1-1 full court zone press. We also work this drill using the same techniques from a 2-1-2 and 2-2-1 full court trapping situation. When the "Knight" drill is used with a 2-1-2 full court trapping situation, we must back up within three and one-half seconds into the 2-1-2 zone. If a 2-2-1 full court trapping situation is used for the "Knight" drill, we must regroup into a 1-2-2 zone within three and one-half seconds. The passer in the full court re-grouping drill releases the ball to the receiver on the coach's command. A coach or manager will use a stopwatch to time the three and one-half second regrouping technique. When three and one-half seconds are up, he will blow his whistle and all players must freeze. When the season starts the players should be able to get into a good defensive stance in his particular zone area by the time three and one-half seconds has elapsed.

Knight Three-Quarter Regrouping Drill

The Knight three-quarter court regrouping drill using a 2-1-2 three-quarter court trapping situation is illustrated in Diagram 9-15.

The offensive receiver is on the ball side of the floor near the sideline, and the passer is inside the double team. As soon as the pass leaves the passer's fingertips, the defense must regroup into the 2-1-2 zone within two and one-half seconds. This is the time limit we feel will not allow our press to be beaten. If a 1-2-1-1 three-quarter court trapping situation is used, we regroup into the 1-3-1 zone within two and one-half seconds. If a 2-2-1 three-quarter court trapping situation is used, we regroup into the 1-2-2 zone.

As in the "Knight" full court regrouping drill, this drill begins with the coach's command, and when the time (2½ seconds) is up, the manager will blow his whistle and the defensive player must freeze. We want them in a good defensive stance in their particular zone area.

Knight Half Court Regrouping Drill

Using a 1-3-1 half court trap regrouping into the 1-3-1 zone as an example, the "Knight" half court trapping drill is shown in Diagram 9-16.

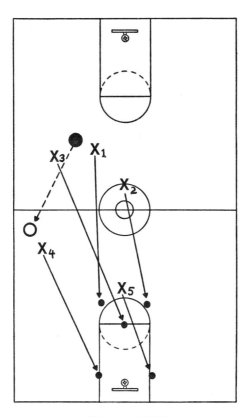

Diagram 9-15

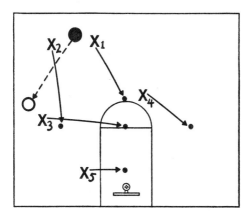

Diagram 9-16

In the half court drill, we want the defenders to be regrouped in good defensive stances in their particular zone areas within one and one-half seconds. If we use a 2-1-2 half court trapping situation, we regroup into the 2-1-2 zone within one and one-half seconds. If we use a 1-2-2 half court trapping situation, we must regroup into the 1-2-2 zone within one and one-half seconds. This regrouping drill begins with the coach's command and ends on the manager's whistle with the players freezing at the spot on the floor where they are.

ONE-ON-ONE DRILLS

One-On-One Overplay Drill

The one-on-one overplay drill (Diagram 9-17) is designed to keep the inbounds receiver from getting the inbounds pass. A manager

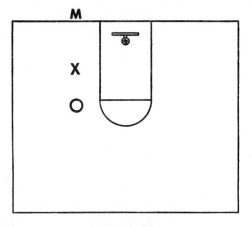

Diagram 9-17

makes the inbounds pass. The defensive man, X, plays between his man, 0, and the basketball. This forces a lob pass to be made to the receiver which is the easiest pass to intercept. The defensive man must establish a position where he can see both the receiver and the man with the basketball. When he sees the ball thrown, he opens to the ball and intercepts the pass. The receiver, 0, is allowed to use only one half the width of the floor and cannot go past the top of the key length-wise. (Diagram 9-18)

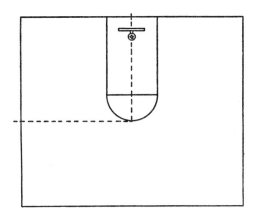

Diagram 9-18

The Dummy Drill

The dummy drill (Diagram 9-19) is a one-on-one defensive drill using three quarters of the floor. We station players, ⊗, at various spots on the floor to act as our defensive dummies. The offensive player, 0, lines up near the hash mark in back court with the defensive player, ⊗, in a good defensive stance about an arm's length away.

The offensive player drives to the basket using the dummies, ⊗, as stationary screens to get rid of the defensive man. The defensive man fights the screens and either steals the ball, causes a turnover, or makes the offensive man give up his dribble. This drill will teach the defensive player how to slide and how to fight screens. The defensive player is allowed to go under the screens in the back court but must go over the top of the screens when the ball crosses half court.

The One-On-One Charge Drill

The one-on-one charge drill (Diagram 9-20) is the defensive drill we use to teach our players to take the charge. This drill will reveal to the coach the players who really want to play. It has definitely helped make my players aggressive.

The offensive player, 0, and the defensive player, X, line up opposite each other at the left and right side of the foul lane. On the coach's whistle 0 dribbles hard across the lane straight towards the defensive player. X meets 0 about half way into the lane and must take the charge.

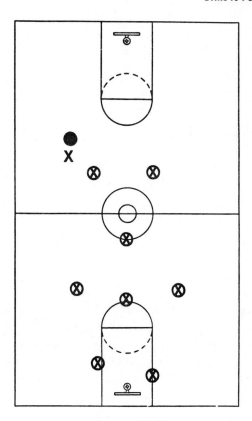

Diagram 9-19

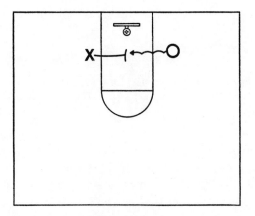

Diagram 9-20

REACTION DRILLS

Reflex Drill

In the reflex drill we divide the squad into groups of twos. One is assigned the role of actor, and the other is the reactor. They stand about three feet apart facing each other. The actor does anything with his hands or feet dealing with movement. The defensive player does everything the actor does as quickly as possible. This is a great drill for the hand and feet reflexes of the defensive players.

Ball Drill

The ball drill is a drill I picked up from coaching football that has really helped me in basketball. We divide the squad into two groups on both ends of the floor with a coach at each group. As individual player will step out of the group with his back turned to the coach, who is about ten feet away. The coach passes the ball to the player and yells "ball" as soon as it is released from his hands. The player turns around quickly and must find the ball and catch it. This reaction drill has helped us make numerous interceptions.

The Hand Reaction Drill

The hand reaction drill is a hand reflex drill we picked up from Jimmy Earle, head basketball coach of Middle Tennessee State University. It is designed to sharpen up a defensive player's hand reflexes and his eye-hand coordination. This drill is used best when the players first come on the floor before the actual practice session begins.

The drill is set up by marking seven spots on the gym wall. The player assumes a basic defensive stance about one and a half or two feet from the wall where the spots are marked. The defensive player, on a whistle by the coach or manager, quickly jabs with his hands and touches three of the marks on the wall by touching them with opposite hand to opposite spot. After he has touched the three spots, he quickly returns to his original defensive position and awaits the next command. On the next command he quickly touches three of the spots he did not touch the time before.

Diagram 9-21 illustrates the illustrates the location of the markings on the wall in the hand reaction drill.

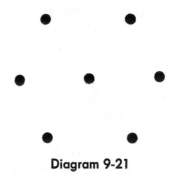

Diagram 9-21

BLOCKING OUT DRILLS

Blocking out for a rebound is a necessary defensive technique at Cumberland College. Our blocking out techniques consist of one-on-one, two-on-two, and three-on-three drills.

One-On-One Blocking Out Drill

Our basic one-on-one blocking out drill is illustrated in Diagram 9-22. The manager can line up to shoot the ball at any area of the floor within fifteen feet of the basket. When the manager shoots, X, the defensive man, will face the basket and block the defender from the basket with his body. He must feel the offensive man with his but-

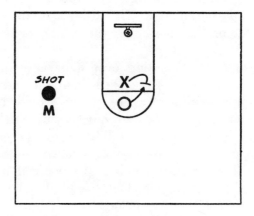

Diagram 9-22

tocks and hands to keep the offensive player from getting in front of him. When the ball comes off the board, the defender must get the ball by ripping it off the boards coming down with the ball in his hands, elbows spread, and feet well apart.

Two-On-Two Block Out Drill

The two-on-two block out drill (Diagram 9-23) uses the same techniques as described in the one-on-one block out drill but congests the lane area more by adding another couple. The offensive men, 0, line up at the corners of the free throw line. The defensive men, X, play between their men and the basket.

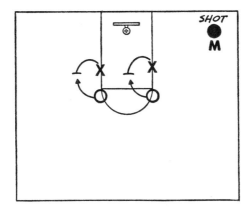

Diagram 9-23

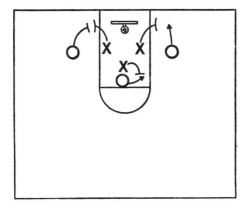

Diagram 9-24

Three-On-Three Block Out Drill

The blocking out drills are now increased to three against three (Diagram 9-24). We emphasize forming our defensive cup around the basket. We use the same blocking out techniques as described in the one-on-one blocking out drill.

All of these drills are very important to us. Although we use most of these drills in the pre-season we also use them during the season. I think we, as coaches, tend to get away from these drills during the season and as we all know through drills our defenses and offenses are perfected. Therefore, we have adopted the philosophy of utilizing these same drills in the middle and latter part of our season and not just before the season. I have found that doing these drills all through the season our presses are much more proficient. We will use these drills throughout the entire season in our future years.

INDEX

A

Attitude, positive, 97-98

B

Backup sliding drill, 190
Backward movement, 18-19
Ball drill, 197
Blocking out drills, 198-200 (see also Drills)
Boxer zone press:
  basic defensive coverages, 129, 130
  left forward, 129
  left guard, 129
  match up with a team, 129
  regrouping, 133
  retreat into 1-2-2 zone defense, 133
  right forward, 129
  right guard, 129
  safety man, 129
  teams used against, 128
  trapper, 129
  2-2-1 alignment, 128, 129
  when calling audibles, 128
Bulldog press:
  against quick teams, 121
  assignments swapped, 126
  ball brought to right side, 123
  ball crosses half court line on dribble, 127
  ball inbounds on left side, 126
  best trapping guard, 122
  center, 122
  change-of-pace, 121
  dribbler, 123
  first forward pass completed, 127
  forwards, 122
  initial alignment, 122
  left guard, 122
  lob pass, 122
  middle man, 122
  opponents bring ball in, 123
  regrouping, 127
  right guard, 122
  slides and coverages, 123, 126
  stunt, 124, 126, 127
  successful trap, 124
  timing, 123
  2-1-2 zone defense, 127, 128
Bulldog Sliding Drill, 188-190

C

Corner trapping drill, 188
Cumberland College, 56

D

Defensing throw-ins, 93-96
Defensive regrouping drills, 191-194 (see also Drills)
Delay attack: half-court, 40-50
Dogging presses:
  advantages, 112
  big man in back, 112
  changing, 111
  conditioning, 112
  double team situation on ball, 112
  gambles not as great, 112
  guards up front, 112
  less physically demanding, 112
  listed, 111
  make opponent attack, 112
  1-2-1-1 three-quarter "Mad-dog" press, 113-121 (see also Mad-dog press)
  opponent not allowed to hold ball, 112
  opponent's poor passing ability, 112
  passing, 112
  placement of personnel, 112
  team with no depth, 112
  term, 111
  2-1-2 three-quarter "Bulldog" press, 121-128 (see also Bulldog press)
  2-2-1 three-quarter "Boxer" press, 128-133 (see also Boxer press)
Drills:
  blocking out, 198-200
    one-on-one, 198-199
    two-on-two, 199
    three-on-three, 200
  defensive regrouping, 191-194
    Knight full court, 191-192
    Knight half court, 192-194
    Knight three-quarter court, 192, 193
  one-on-one, 194-196
    charge, 195-196
    dummy, 195, 196
    overplay, 194
  reaction, 197
    ball, 197